A Dream of Giants

The Story of the Sunshine Coast Trail

by Emma Levez Larocque

This book is dedicated to Eagle Walz, Scott Glaspey, and all the people who have helped to make the Sunshine Coast Trail what it is today.

Contents

Foreword

Recreation trails continue to be a hot topic at many discussion tables responsible for tourism, economic development, community health and sustainability. The undeniable benefits of such trails have been well documented and include the preservation of eco-sensitive areas, the promotion of healthy lifestyles, their proven ability to increase property values, the list goes on. But one important benefit that is less often published is a trail's ability to pull together an entire community, instilling a sense of unwavering pride within the hearts of trail builders, supporters and recreational users. This is a benefit which surfaces well before the first pair of boots even hit the dirt. I am referring to camaraderie.

This insightful book showcases just that. How a simple vision, coupled with not-so-simple volunteer manual labour, can lead to the development of a trail that is gaining international attention as an unforgettable "bucket list" experience; the Sunshine Coast Trail. The trail itself is magical, no doubt. With panoramic ocean views, pristine coastal lakes, plunging rivers and waterfalls, towering coastal mountains, beautiful old-growth forest, bridges and bluffs, the trail is engagingly diverse and certainly unforgettable. It is, however, the history of its conception that provides the real story and Emma's book is an honest account of the blood, sweat and tears of those who believe in the power of connecting people with nature, and in turn, with each other. Instead of solely showcasing the obvious beauty of the Sunshine Coast Trail from a user's perspective, she celebrates the efforts of the people responsible for giving this trail to the users who benefit from its existence.

I recall the first time I met Emma. In fact, she was one of the first people I met when I moved to the Sunshine Coast in 2009. We share a similar passion for photography and the outdoors, and I've had the pleasure of working with her in both realms. Emma's contribution, through this book, is a vital part of the Sunshine Coast camaraderie that continues to move mountains, or at the very least provide the pathways that put hikers directly on top of them.

Enjoy!

Darren Robinson

Executive Director, Tourism Powell River
Director, Sunshine Coast Tourism
Photographer, Darren Robinson Photography

Cortes Island

Red Cedar

Orcas

Arbutus

Bald Eagle

Hernando Island

Copeland Islands

Savary Island

Marbled Murrelet

Sarah Point

Wednesday Lake

Lund

Manzanita Bluffs

OKEOVER INLET

Rieveley's Pond

Appleton Creek

Kayach Bluffs

Gibraltar Bluff

Sliammon Lakes

Sliammon

Spawning Salmon

Powell River

Harwood Island

Texada Island

Blackberry

N

Legend

▨ Park or Protected Area	━━ Sunshine Coast Trail	🏞 Bluff	
····· Ferry Route	★ Trail head	🌄 View Point	
━━ Highway	🏠 Shelter or Cabin	🌉 Bridge	
----- Gravel / 4x4 Road	🌲 Old Growth Forest	🏊 Swimming Area	
▭▭ Canoe Route	🏡 B&B	💧 Waterfall	

Goat Island

Manzanita

Goat Lake

Banana Slug

Rhododendron

Sword Ferns

Salal

Red Squirrel

Cougar

Powell Lake

Fiddlehead Landing

Tin Hat Mtn.

Windsor Lake

Lois River

Giavanno Lake

Confederation Lake

Slide Bluff

Lewis Lake

Ireland Lake

Dodd Lake

Inland Lake

Lost Lake

Haslam Lake

March Lake

Elk Lake

Nanton Lake

Horseshoe Lake

Freda Creek

Khartoum Lake

Ladyslipper

Duck Lake

Granite Lake

Walt Hill

Swabian Bluffs

Elk

Lois Lake

Elephant Lakes

Mt. Troubridge

Nelson Bluff

Rainy Day Lakes

Bull Frog

HOTHAM SOUND

Lang Bay

Lake Bluff

Herondell B&B

Saltery Bay

Fairview Bay

JERVIS INLET

Nelson Island

9

A Seed is Planted

The Sunshine Coast Trail began as a dream, as many wonderful things do. The vision, dedication and hard work it has taken to make that dream a reality is not easy to comprehend. It has been a labour of love – a 180-kilometre-long project almost 20 years in the making. It winds through a history of land, tells the story of a people, showcases an area of extreme and delicate beauty, and harbours the echoes of much laughter and the camaraderie that has nurtured its development.

The seed for the Sunshine Coast Trail was planted, ironically, in a clear-cut. Eagle Walz, whose name is now synonymous with the Sunshine Coast Trail and hiking in Powell River, was driving north from his home to Lund. It was 1992.

"One day I saw this cutblock along the side of the road. It wasn't huge at all – maybe 50 metres wide by about 200 metres. It looked so out of place. It was the first time I had seen logging up close, and that tweaked my interest. I thought, 'Oh Geez, what's going on here?' I started looking into it. Until that time I didn't know that a person could actually go for a walk in a Crown forest. I always thought it was something that belonged to someone, and that I would be trespassing, even though I knew it was Crown land. When I found out differently, I started thinking. I was interested in big trees and I started looking for big trees."

It didn't take long for Eagle to realize that the big trees that were left in this area were disappearing in a big hurry, and he was concerned about it.

"It didn't seem like we should have the same thing happening here that happened with the cedars of Lebanon. In the Lebanese Mountains they had vast forests of 1,000-year-old cedars with incredible girth in biblical times, and they're all but gone today." An elementary school teacher and father to two daughters, he wanted to find a way to protect as much of the old growth that was left as possible so that future generations would still have stands of ancient forests left to enjoy. But what people cannot see they often do not care about.

"We realized that the only way of getting people interested in the goal of wanting to save those trees was to get them out there to see them. And the only way to get them there was to build a trail, so that's what we started to do. We started doing the research to find out where these patches of old growth were in the backcountry and looking for a way of connecting them, and that's how the Sunshine Coast Trail came to be."

Firm Friends

Scott Glaspey is a key part of that "we". It's a friendship that has been forged over years of campfires and smokies, a bond that has been cemented with "crazy" plans of the daunting feat of building a marathon trail through difficult terrain, not to mention a mountain range. These two, with the help of many others along the way, have literally moved boulders together.

"I always say that Eagle tricked me into fixing a trail with him," Scott says. "It was the Sliammon Lakes section. He said, 'If we could connect this little section here, we could have two trails that fit together, and wouldn't that be great.' So we got out there and started working on it, and I found that I really liked it."

In 1992 Eagle, Scott and a handful of others formed the Powell River Parks and Wilderness Society (PRPAWS) with the goal of setting aside protected wilderness areas. The idea of building an epic trail to do this was formed early on.

"Eagle and I would often be working on trails, staying in the bush overnight. We'd be sleeping out somewhere and we'd have a campfire, and somehow this long trail idea came up. At that point we had 20 kilometres strung together. We realized that if we made one more connection we would have 30." They kept hearing about the West Coast Trail, which is 78 kilometres long, so that was the distance to beat. "Within three or four years we had pretty well gone from Sarah Point to Fiddlehead Farm – that

(right) Eagle Walz doing maintenance on the East Mount Troubridge Trail.

was 81 kilometres. Now we realized we could go all the way to Saltery Bay, and we just decided to go nuts."

"Nuts" was the right word for it, according to some local forestry employees. "Some of the forestry guys told us we'd never build a trail through the Smith Range," Scott laughs his big laugh. "And we said, 'You just watch us!' It got ridiculous, but it has happened. We had a couple of grants along the way, but they were only responsible for about 35 kilometres, so we've built about 145 kilometres of trail, and 80 per cent of the work has been done by volunteers."

Making a Plan

A lot of the work connected with the Sunshine Coast Trail has taken place in the actual building of the trail, out in the forests, up and down hills and valleys and mountains. The result of that work is highly visible to the general public. But innumerable hours have also gone into planning, meetings, reports, document writing – all the somewhat less glamorous background work. From an early stage there was a plan, an actual business plan, as a matter of fact.

Scott Glaspey and Eagle Walz enjoying a day out on the trails.

"The business plan gave voice to our notion that in order for the trail to succeed in being more than a flash in the pan, it had to show that it could create wealth," Eagle says. "It had to show that there were economic benefits to having this infrastructure for recreation and tourism in place for the diversification of our local economy. Having the business plan, and having it researched by independent researchers, gave it legitimacy and helped promote the idea that the project was possible." PRPAWS has been following that business plan for almost 20 years.

It Takes a Community to Build a Trail

This book is not meant to give a trail-by-trail description; you can find that in Eagle Walz's invaluable guidebook entitled *The Sunshine Coast Trail*. Rather, it is meant to highlight events, features, and stories that per-

tain to various parts of the trail. It aspires to communicate a sense of the magnificent achievement that is the Sunshine Coast Trail, and invite you to get involved if you can, by becoming part of the community that is necessary to complete, maintain, and protect it.

A Dream of Giants: The Story of the Sunshine Coast Trail is divided into the five successive trail sections that have been identified by PRPAWS, travelling from north to south. It is my hope that as you explore its pages you will be inspired to hike the trail, if you haven't already, and to appreciate this great gift that Eagle, Scott, the longtime members of the PRPAWS executive board, and all the many people who have helped along the way have given to the Powell River community.

Old Growth Forests

Old growth forests are woods of great age that exhibit unique biological features. Most of the old growth trees in the Powell River area are either Western redcedar, Western hemlock, Yellow cedar or Douglas fir, for which old growth is considered to be 250 years or older. Old growth forests are important not only for their spiritual and economic value, but also because they enable biodiversity, providing homes to a wide variety of plants and animals, many of which cannot live in younger forests.

The First Leg
Sarah Bay to Malaspina Road

¤ Land's End Trail
¤ Gwendoline Hills Trail

A Good Start

The Sunshine Coast Trail officially begins where the land ends at Sarah Point. Although it's possible to drive almost all the way to the trailhead in a hardy 4x4 vehicle, it's worth the experience to park in Lund and arrive at the beginning of the trail via water taxi. At Sarah Bay you will get your first taste of the magical experience that lies ahead of you. The Land's End Trail is a favourite for many local hikers, weaving as it does along the coastline and affording spectacular views and close encounters with the ocean's edge that are only common on this and the Fairview Bay Trail, at the southernmost end of the SCT.

The Parks of Land's End

To the northeast, Malaspina Peninsula, on which the Land's End and Gwendoline Hills trails are located, borders Desolation Sound Marine Provincial Park. This park was established in 1973 "to protect an isolated area of safe boating waters, surrounding inlets and islands and a natural marine environment at the head of Georgia Strait" (BC Parks).

Desolation Sound, a well-loved destination for boaters, got its uncomplimentary name from the British explorer, Captain George Vancouver, who first sailed the area in 1792. If you are visiting on a sunny day it's difficult to imagine how the name ever crossed Vancouver's mind; but during a cold, wet spell, it might be easier. In his book, *A Voyage of Discovery to the North Pacific Ocean and Round the World, 1791-1795*, Vancouver describes his June arrival in the area as "dark and rainy." He couldn't imagine any animal or plant thriving on the desolate shores. Today, however, Desolation Sound Marine Provincial Park, which encompasses 8,449 hectares and the three major destination anchorages Prideaux Haven, Tenedo's Bay and Grace Harbour, is a yachter's paradise.

Another park in this area, Malaspina Provincial Park, was established in 2001. It is comprised of a strip of land along the northern and eastern shore of Malaspina Peninsula, and includes the first 15 kilometres of the SCT.

(far left) Eagle enjoys a chilly but spectacular walk near Sarah Point ~ Margot Glaspey photo; (above) Cochrane Bay is one of the beautiful spots you can access from the Land's End Trail; (right) Pacific harbour seals are curious, and have been known to follow hikers as they traverse the oceanside sections of this trail.

Pacific harbour seal *(Phoca vitulina)*

If you are lucky you may spot one of these inquisitive creatures watching you as you walk along a shore section of the Land's End Trail. Pacific harbour seals are the most common type of seal found in temperate waters. They live north of the equator in both the Atlantic and Pacific oceans. The adult Pacific harbour seal may reach a length of 1.6 to 1.9 metres and weigh between 60 and 120 kilograms. Their colour can range from brownish to black, with a speckled pattern. Pacific harbor seals spend about half their time on land and the other half in the water. They can dive to 300 metres for up to 40 minutes, and they sometimes sleep in the water (Marine Mammal Center).

Wednesday Lake, named for the Wednesday Hikers, is a favourite spot for tired feet to rest.

This park was negotiated by PRPAWS, and came about as part of the Protected Area Strategy, which was a provincial initiative that aimed to set aside 12 per cent of land as park space throughout the province.

 "On behalf of PRPAWS I was negotiating with the forest companies and government organizations for the creation of Inland Lake Provincial Park," Eagle explains. "The area we were talking about also extended to and included the top end of Haslam Lake. It would have been a very nice-sized park." Because it would limit access to wood on the west side of Haslam Lake, however, the forest companies involved wouldn't agree to the inclusion of the Haslam section. So Eagle suggested applying the hectares that didn't make it into Inland Lake Provincial Park toward the establishment of a park around the beginning of the first section of the SCT on Malaspina Peninsula. After much negotiation everyone at the table agreed and both Inland Lake Provincial Park and, a little later, Malaspina Provincial Park were formed.

When a part of the trail is guaranteed protection, it's exciting, and a huge relief, Eagle says. "I feel like all this work that we're doing is paying off, and that the vision of having a ribbon of old growth in 100 years or so is after all a possible outcome. By having the trail protected – in Malaspina Park for instance – those first 15 kilometres are now growing older by the day, and they will not be logged. The same is true for Inland Lake. There, another 20 kilometres or so of trail will be protected. It's a wonderful experience, and that's really what we're working to do."

Hut-to-Hut Hiking

Several lovely views lie in wait on the Gwendoline Hills Trail. Perhaps the most impressive is from Manzanita Bluffs, which is the site of the first hut you will encounter if you are travelling along the trail in a southerly direction.

The concept of a hut-to-hut hiking experience on the SCT started percolating when Scott and his wife Margot visited New Zealand and did some multi-day hiking where a hut was the destination of each day's trek. They

(right) The bright bark of an Arbutus tree.

returned to Powell River, with the seed of an idea. It took a few years for Scott and Eagle to figure out how to make that seed grow, but they knew they wanted to find a way to make it possible.

Jim Stutt is a local general contractor who had been involved with PRPAWS on a casual basis for a number of years when discussion of the huts began.

"Eagle and I were up at the very tail end of what was left of Fiddlehead Farm. There is a little woodshed there with a little bit of a gable roof and posts. We were lounging in there on one of our hikes having a sandwich, and he started asking, 'How much would it cost to build something like this?' I started thinking, and evolving in my mind what it would look like."

In the fall of 2009, PRPAWS received provincial funding through the Island Coastal Economic Trust (ICET) to build eight huts in various locations along the trail. The $160,000 from ICET had to be matched by an equivalent amount of in-kind volunteer labour and other donations and funding sources. The trust has put funding into a number of trails on Vancouver Island and the Sunshine Coast because it sees them as a great vehicle for economic development.

CEO Al Baronas says one of the things that drew ICET's attention to the SCT is that individual hikers can do as much, or as little, of the trail as they choose. "It's a difficult trail, but it's criss-crossed with roads so you don't have to do the whole 180 kilometres. Lots of people will not be able to do that distance, but they will be able to do segments. Another thing that gives the trail appeal is the eight huts. Those huts make it extra special."

Once the hut prototype at Fairview Bay at the southern end of the SCT was built, there was no looking back. Jim's role became critical at this point, as he designed the huts and provided direction to a crew of eager, but somewhat inexperienced, builders. Each hut is unique: some are open, some are full cabins, but they are all rooted in a basic design.

"I designed the huts thinking that at some point we could have finished cabins all along the trail," Jim says. "Being that we only had so much money, this allowed us to maintain the greatest amount of flexibility."

(far left) Hikers returning from the opening at Manzanita Hut; (left) Moss reclaims a rusty car for the forest; (below) This picturesque spot along the Gwendoline Hills Trail gives a different view of Wednesday Lake.

PRPAWS Board Member Bob Davey hangs the comment box at 3K Bluffs as the site at Emil's Bench is completed. ~ Eagle Walz photo

Emil's Bench

On 3K Bluff sits one of the many PRPAWS benches that are dotted along the Sunshine Coast Trail. This is Emil's Bench, in memory of a logging contractor named Emil Krompocker.

With the placement and naming of this bench PRPAWS paid homage to Emil, who showed foresight when he logged the area several decades ago, leaving a lot of the old growth Douglas fir trees intact and protected. "Apparently the trees where too big to take out," Eagle explains, "but loggers were told to drop the giants nevertheless. Emil said no. The trees continue to grow – his legacy to us."

It's a fine sight to behold, and a good subject for contemplation, as you enjoy the view of magnificent old growth trees from Emil's Bench.

A Team, and a Leader

A monumental effort from many people over the span of two years has made the building of seven of the eight huts possible (2009-2011). The last hut is slated for construction in 2012. The importance of Jim's role in this stage of the trail's development cannot be overstated, Eagle says.

"Jim's participation in this as the 'lead building guy' has been indispensable. For us to try and have done it without Jim would have been far less efficient, and far less inspiring also. We would have stayed with a very simple construction that would have been replicated elsewhere with fewer changes. His role as a mentor on the job has been just fabulous, and he's enjoyed working with all different groups, like the BOMB Squad, the Rotary and the ATV clubs, apart from just the PRPAWS board and other regular participants. He's gotten to know a lot of people and has been able to share his expertise with them in a way that makes everyone feel at ease."

During the building of the cabin close to the summit of Tin Hat Mountain Jim's ability to communicate what needed to be done really shone through after he injured his hand and was unable to do much of the actual work. Eagle laughs: "He is there, like a director in a movie, or a conductor, waving his wand. And there, a few weeks later, is a cabin!"

Bob Davey, one of the newer members of the PRPAWS executive, talks about being involved with the building of the huts. "You learn a lot without even really realizing that you're learning. Jim's a really good teacher and overseer. He can see the whole site while he's working away at something. He'll anticipate that someone is going to come up with an issue and get someone else to help. You don't even realize that you're learning, but all of a sudden you go, 'Hey, look what I just did!'"

(right) The Grand Opening of the Manzanita Hut in June 2011 was a huge success with more than 160 people in attendance.

here at malaspina
between green hills
and the sea
i've laid bricks
turned the earth
the rainworms
in my garden
here at malaspina
i have watched gulls
write coded messages
and here
between green hills
and the sea
here at malaspina
rainbow-rich and gull
hungry
i've decoded the flight
of gulls
words
keep falling
in my hands
summery snowflakes
in a hovering
i see you
here at malaspina
between green hills
and the sea

~ Eagle Walz

(above) A view from the Gwendoline Hills Trail; (right) Betty Wilson gives a First Nation's blessing at the opening of Manzanita Hut.

A Grand Opening to Remember

The Manzanita Hut was the fifth of the eight huts to be constructed, and in June 2011 a grand opening made a big statement about the impact these new amenities will have on the future of the trail. Eagle remembers the lead-up to the event with a delighted chuckle.

"Seeing that the Manzanita Hut is located in a fairly remote place for the average person, we knew that a lot of people wouldn't be able to get to it. Thanks to Island Timberlands agreeing to let us use their road to allow closer access to the hut, we were able to get more people in. To begin with I thought if we could get 40 or 50 people that would be great. Maybe in our wildest dreams we would get 60 to 80. Then on the day, it rained in town, and I thought, well, 30 or 40 maybe. But the weather started breaking. Then I got to the trailhead and I saw all those cars – more than 50! It was thrilling to see that many people there, and by the time they were ready to go I thought to myself, we could have as many as 80 people, or maybe even close to 100! Well, as it turned out there were numbers who accessed it from the cutblock, the short way. To see 160 people all make their way up there, it was a real thrill."

Manzanita *(Arctostaphylos)*

Manzanita is a common name for many species of the genus *Arctostaphylos*. Manzanita shrubs are found on this section of the Sunshine Coast Trail, and especially near Manzanita Bluffs. Related to the Arbutus tree, manzanitas are evergreen shrubs or small trees that are characterized by smooth reddish-brown bark that flakes and peels, and stiff, twisting branches. They bloom in winter and early spring and carry berries in the spring and summer. Their name means "little apples" in Spanish. *(Plants of the Pacific Northwest Coast* by J. Pojar and A. MacKinnon)

Warming Up
Malaspina Road to Powell Lake

¤ Thunder Ridge Trail
¤ Toquenatch Trail
¤ Marathon Trail
¤ Appleton Canyon Trail
¤ Sliammon Lakes Trail
¤ Scout Mountain Trail

A World of Green

The first trail in this section is Thunder Ridge, and though it is relatively short, it has several highlights that make it memorable. Keep your eyes open for some substantial Douglas fir trees, and artefacts that are remnants of early logging in the area. About 15 minutes in you will come across Fern Creek, a picturesque spot nestled in a little valley, and adorned by a small wooden bridge and set of stairs. The Fullers, who owned the woodlot licence in this area until recently, left their mark by designing their cutblocks to ensure generous trail buffers. These accommodations preserved the green lushness found on the Thunder Ridge Trail today. This section of the trail is now part of the proposed Sliammon Treaty Settlement Lands.

Shuffle to Support the Sunshine Coast Trail

The Marathon Shuffle, a 29-kilometre walk/run, is an annual rite of spring in Powell River. It is at Thunder Ridge (from Malaspina Road) that this event begins. The shuffle, which includes everything from Thunder Ridge Trail to the end of Scout Mountain Trail, has been held each year since 1993. The event was started to help raise awareness about the SCT, and to get more people out to experience it. Participation has grown steadily, and in recent years the shuffle has attracted a number of people from the Lower Mainland and Vancouver Island, other provinces, and even the United States.

"Shuffle" is somewhat misleading as an event description, though everyone is encouraged to participate at his/her own ability level. There are hikers who bring their lunches and truly "shuffle," but many people run it as a race. The fastest time recorded to date is held by Powell River runner Kevin Sigouin, who ran it in 2 hours, 57 minutes and 13 seconds in the 2009 event. It must be understood by people who have not participated in the shuffle or travelled these sections of the SCT, this is no ordinary marathon. Of course the distance is less, but the terrain is much more challenging than an average marathon. Up and down hills large and small, in and out of gullies you go, all the while passing some of the most spectacular scenery the area has to offer. It's a great introduction to Powell River's backcountry and the SCT, and is sure to leave participants wanting more. Several years ago a 12-kilometre "half shuffle" was added as an option for those who wanted to participate, but did not wish to tackle the entire distance.

The Ghost of Old Gnarly

Until a few years ago, the Thunder Ridge section was home to one of the largest old-growth Douglas fir trees accessible to the public on this stretch of coast. It was more than 2.5 metres in diameter, and estimated to be 1,000 years old. Because of its gnarled appearance, it became known as "Old Gnarly." When British Columbia Forest Service (BCFS) announced that the area was to be logged, PRPAWS set to work trying to protect the old giant.

"We tried to negotiate a buffer around Old Gnarly because standing there in isolation we thought it would blow over," Eagle explains. "While BCFS promised that they would leave some trees, no surrounding trees were left at all by the logging contractor. It was an old tree; it had rot inside, and it could not withstand the storms. Within a couple of years of being all on its own and not having the protection of the surrounding forest, it was gone.

(left) A mossy hike on the Thunder Ridge section; (left, inset) The beginning of the Marathon Shuffle; (right) Fern Creek is one of the treasures of this trail.

(above) An old oxen skidroad, on which oxen and loggers once hauled logs from the woods to the ocean, now makes up part of the Toquenatch Trail ~ photo courtesy of the Powell River Forestry Museum; (inset) A current-day view of the Toquenatch Trail; (far right) A pretty waterfall along this trail section; (far right, inset) Wildflowers provide a colourful splash amongst vibrant greens.

It collapsed due to the winds and due to its age, but it would have stood there for another 100 years or longer had it had the protection of a mature forest around it that reached almost as high as itself. But they wouldn't give us a buffer around it. That was very disappointing to me."

When Eagle found out that Old Gnarly was gone, it seemed he had lost an old friend.

"Someone told me that it had fallen down. I went out there and was washed with disappointment. It was special. There are special things all along, and someone looking at it from a different point of view might say, 'Well everything's special to you, just get over it. There's still lots of special left.' But that was the biggest tree in the Powell River area accessible to people."

It was one of the disappointments in the years of ups and downs that have made up the experience of building, and rebuilding, the SCT. Attitudes are changing slowly, Eagle says, and that's one of the rewards.

"That sort of attitude – 'I'm taking whatever I want' – is changing. Times change. It's gotten easier to convince logging companies and contractors to give some consideration to values other than just timber extraction. Still, it continues to be a struggle."

Rumbles of the Past

Toquenatch Trail was the first part of the SCT to be established by PRPAWS. Much of it winds along an old skidroad, so it is wide and mossy, and incredibly green all year round. It was built first because it was in Eagle's neighborhood, and it was close to an existing trail that had been built by the BOMB Squad.

"I thought, why not make a longer trail," Eagle says. "So we built a new gently graded trail, along upper Toquenatch Creek and hooked into the Marathon Trail where it levels out and turns toward Gibraltar. Toquenatch had an old historical skidroad bed and a beautiful creek, and it was easy to build on that, not knowing how to build a trail when I began."

(above) Some impressive Douglas fir trees can be seen along the Toquenatch Trail; (right) Take the time to stop at the many magical spots along this trail.

Douglas fir (Pseudotsuga menziesii)

The second-tallest conifer in the world, Douglas fir is the most common tree species in the Powell River area. Fir grows from sea level to areas of roughly 800-metres elevation, and old growth fir can be up to 90 metres tall, 3 metres in diameter, and 800 years old. These trees are important food and habitat sources for birds and animals at every stage of their lifecycle. Among other things, Douglas fir seedlings are an important food source for Black-tailed Deer and elk in winter months; the seeds are favorite snacks of small animals like voles, mice, shrews and chipmunks; and older trees and snags provide primary habitat for the Spotted Owl. Look for the Toquenatch Fir, which is labeled at the southern end of Toquenatch Trail, for a good example of beautiful old growth Douglas fir.

If you stand still and listen quietly you can almost hear the rumble of the past trying to catch up with you. Once you climb down the hill from Plummer Creek Road, you amble along the remnants of the old oxen skidroad. An excerpt from a display at the Powell River Forestry Museum, written by Rudi van Zwaaij, recreates what the scene would have looked like 120 years ago:

The teams of [oxen, and later horses] used skidroads to drag the logs from the bush to the water, where they would be rafted and towed to the markets. Swampers were the men responsible for building the skidroads and clearing the bush and stumps. Skidders then came along to imbed, at regular intervals, the crosswise poles referred to as the skids.

The bark was peeled off the logs to make them slide easier on the skids. Snipers used their axes to shape the lead end of the logs pencil like, to make the logs ride the skids and not create hang-ups. The Grease Monkey smeared all the logs with lard, whale oil or crude oil to make them easier for the bulls to pull the logs over.

The Doggers drove large steel eyelets called 'dogs' into each log, so chains could be pulled through to link the huge logs together. The biggest logs were always in front, jerking the smaller ones behind.

The man in charge of a bull-team was the Bull-Puncher. Possessor of an impressive vocabulary of profane and abusive words, he was the most feared and respected man in the woods. His job was to keep the bulls working, using his 'goad' or sharp rod to prod the bulls.

Once the string of logs was hooked up to the bulls, the Bull-Puncher yells, "Giddap" and "Hiyaaahh," followed by a string of obscenities to get the bulls underway. Yoked and chained together the big bulls tug and strain at the huge logs. The men help by rolling the timber with cant hooks.

At the end of the string of logs is attached a hollow log, called the 'pig,' containing the tools, chains and dogs. The Pigman rides it down to the water where he collects all the logs and chains. The pig is then pulled back to the woods by the bulls, but in this case is ridden only by the Bull-Puncher to show off his status.

Adopt the pace of nature: her secret is patience. ~ Ralph Waldo Emerson

But there is more history here than goes back 120 years. The area that Toquenatch Trail runs through is traditional Tla'Amin (Sliammon) First Nation territory. A small village was located at the mouth of Toquenatch Creek where, for hundreds, perhaps even thousands, of years, families have come to catch and smoke fish, and to gather plants and medicines for their people. It is one of many sacred places for the Tla'Amin people, and today there is a sweat lodge close to that original site, and very close to the Toquenatch Trail.

John Louie is the men's support counselor at Tla'Amin Community Health. It is his job to care for people who take part in the sweats, and to impart some knowledge and understanding of traditional customs and wisdom to younger First Nations people while they are doing so. The new sweat lodge has been in this location for only a year or so, but it's the history and respect for the land that drew them back to that spot, John says.

"Part of the reason we built the sweat lodge here is that we need to have a presence here. This creek carries a lot of life. That's why we're down here; we want to take that integrity back for this land. People don't know what was here. For me bringing the lodge here is to put that respect back. All we ask is that other people respect it too. We have been bypassed for a long time, and our lands have been desecrated. We were taught to share things amongst our own people. We have to protect and teach our young ones what this all means."

Though the sweat lodge is an interesting detour from the trail, when sessions are in progress, please be respectful and stay away. When people go there and make a lot of noise or are disrespectful, it's disruptive, Louie explains. "For me there are a lot of spirits here. When I come here I announce myself. Wherever people find a place that is a sweat lodge or a sacred area, all we ask is that they respect it."

Toquenatch Trail is magical. You can imagine mythical creatures of all kinds hiding behind the mossy trees or underneath gargantuan ferns, waiting for you to pass. The area is rich with wildlife; Toquenatch Creek is a salmon stream, and favoured habitat for otter too. Waterfalls, bridges, some old growth, and plenty of mature second growth are all features you can admire along this stretch.

The sign on the tree reads: TOQUENACH FALLS BRIDGE 2.1KM / MALASPINA ROAD 7.4KM

THE BOMB Squad

For more than 20 years, the BOMB (Bloody Old Men's Brigade) Squad has been building and maintaining trails and bridges in the Powell River area. Though a separate group from PRPAWS, and mainly active in the Duck Lake area, the contribution they have made to the SCT is important. PRPAWS recognizes the BOMB Squad as a significant ally; many of the bridges found along the SCT are BOMB Squad creations.

The top section of the Marathon Trail was the first trail "officially" built by this team of retired men, which started out with five members, and has included dozens over the years. There were a couple of catalysts that led to the formation of the group. Roger Taylor, one of the BOMB Squad founders, now 91 and still an active member of the group, tells the story.

"I guess it was about 1988 we started. There was one friend, Tony Mathews, who was building a trail from his place at Mowat Bay right through to Haywire Bay. He was doing it on his own. He came to a creek, and all it had was some old planks, which were dicey to walk on; you almost needed to have caulk boots. So he asked us if we would give him a hand. There were three of us: Jim Koleszar, Roy Hewitt and I. So we went up to give him a hand and we built the crossing across the creek."

They enjoyed themselves so much that they knew they were on to something. Then they became aware of John Hooper, who was also doing some trail

Roger estimates that the BOMB Squad has built close to 100 bridges, large and small, and countless kilometres of trail in the Powell River area. Many of the group's efforts have been concentrated in the Duck Lake area. If you haven't already explored such treasures as Sweetwater Trail, Mud Lake Trail or Suicide Creek Trail, get yourself a map of the BOMB Squad trails from Tourism Powell River, and go exploring.

building. He had just completed the Hooper Loop, south of Powell River. Roy Hewitt picks up the story.

"The next thing that happened, was that Helmut Godau and I were driving down Southview Road one day. We noticed on the mountainside beside the road there was a bluff, some cliffs, and it was obviously flat on top, and Helmut said, 'I'd love to get up there.' So we went back the next week, parked where we had seen it, and went across a long valley, which had been logged. It was a heck of a struggle to get through, logs and bits every which way. Lo and behold we came out on a road. We followed the road to the right, which did a hairpin bend, and then it finished at the edge of the clearing that had been logged, and we found a trail going off into the bush.

It was a two-track trail, so obviously a vehicle of some kind. We found later that there had been a homesteader very close by who had built a six-wheel drive vehicle. I had never heard of that before. We had bumped into this trail accidentally so we followed it.

"But several miles up it turned off the wrong way. We wanted to go the other way, so we went cross-country in very rough country. The underbrush was 10-feet high and we were struggling, so we turned back and

(far left) Early members of the BOMB Squad celebrate the completion of the BOMB Squad Bridge on Sweetwater Trail ~ Walter Kubany photo; (left inset) Roger Taylor sets up a makeshift workstation; (below) More recent BOMB Squad members with another beautiful bridge creation. ~ photos courtesy of Roy Hewitt

went home. But we didn't give up! The next week we went back with five guys, and that was the beginning of the BOMB Squad. We made it right through to behind where the cliff was, and we came out on that bluff, which we called Gibraltar, a reminder of our Navy days. We kept going back every Thursday, the five of us, and we made a complete loop trail. We called it the Marathon Trail because one of our members, Roger Taylor, ran marathons."

The Marathon Trail features a long, uphill section that passes through a lovely stand of second growth forest, with several rewards to reap at the top. If you are hiking on a clear day, be sure to carry on to Gibraltar Bluffs and Gentle David for magnificent view of the Toquenatch Valley, Okeover Inlet and the lowlands toward Powell River, with the Strait of Georgia and various islands in the distance. In the spring keep your eyes open for chocolate lilies and lady slippers along this trail.

Rieveley's Pond, named after the hiker, Bill Rieveley, who led hikes for the Wednesday Walkers into his 80th year, is another spot you won't want to miss. A serene, peaceful place to stop for lunch or a break, Rieveley's Pond now also boasts the second of the new huts along the SCT, which the BOMB Squad built with PRPAWS. This hut had its first guests before it was even completed. One morning the building crew showed up to work to find a couple of bleary-eyed hikers who had been caught in snow the night before.

(left) Richie Tait, a longtime hiker, PRPAWS board member and BOMB Squad member, motors through the Marathon trail section during the Marathon Shuffle; (left, above) The hut at Rieveley's Pond was a joint effort between PRPAWS and the BOMB Squad; (right) Gibraltar Bluffs feels like the top of the world on a sunny day.

Gentle David

A beautiful name for a beautiful spot, Gentle David was named by Helmut Godau, for Roy Hewitt's son, David, after David died at the age of 27. "Helmut and I were sitting on Gentle David talking about David and that's how it came to be called that," Roy explains. "It was Helmut's idea. He was the poet of the BOMB Squad. It was his idea to call it Gentle David."

Your deepest roots are in nature. No matter who you are, where you live, or what kind of life you lead, you remain irrevocably linked with the rest of creation. ~ Charles Cook

The Land of A Thousand Tarns

When you ask locals to name their favourite section of the SCT, Appleton Creek often comes up first. Featuring a succession of picturesque waterfalls and some notable old growth trees, this accessible trail is the place to go if you have visitors to impress, and half a day to do it in.

"What's unique about Appleton is that you are always within hearing distance of the creek and the falls, and the soundscape continually changes," Eagle says. "The waterfalls rise from what I call the land of a thousand tarns. There are a lot of little ponds and lakes up in a flat area at the very top of the Bunster Hills. It's all wetlands at an elevation of 3,000 to 4,000 feet, in Yellow cedar country. There's a fair bit of Old Growth Management Area up there, and some Marbled Murrelet nesting sites. It's not part of the SCT, but that's where the water for the waterfalls along the Appleton Creek Trail comes from."

Regardless of the season, you are guaranteed to see some beautiful scenery along this stretch of trail. In the coldest spells of winter the waterfalls freeze over, and the area is transformed into a white wonderland. When the water is rushing in spring you can stand next to Gorge Falls, the largest of the falls along the trail, and the force of the water will take your breath away, literally! In summer, Appleton Creek provides a cool, refreshing place to rejuvenate, and as fall approaches the waters begin to rise again.

Geocaching

Geocaching is a popular activity around the world, and Powell River is no exception. Defined by www.geocaching.com as "a real-world, hi-tech outdoor treasure hunting game," participants hide geocaches (containers with small treasures inside) anywhere they dream up, and register the GPS coordinates and a clue about the cache with geocaching.com for others to find. The idea is to encourage people to explore places they might not have otherwise visited, using the clues and a GPS, or GPS-enabled device. There are several geocaches along the Sunshine Coast Trail. Try it out and find a fun, new way to explore, or hide a cache of your own.

Troll Bridge

Not long after entering Sliammon Lakes Trail you will come upon a charming footbridge that crosses a small creek. It bears a sign that tells you its name: Troll Bridge. This is indeed a place under which you could imagine a small, but friendly, troll living. Eagle remembers naming this bridge, with a smile.

"I used to take my girls for a hike, and Troll Bridge was a half hour hike from the road. Getting to water is always interesting for adults, and certainly to children, and they would bring their Barbies along when we went there. Their Barbies went swimming and they had their house, and there were trolls and a stump in which one troll lived, and another troll was underneath the bridge." The trolls were in fact real – small troll dolls that Eagle's daughters had brought there because – well, it seems such an appropriate place for trolls to be. "One of the trolls lived there for some time until the water, or some other child took it away," Eagle says. And so it became Troll Bridge.

Good Neighbours

The Sliammon Lakes Trail is located on proposed Tla'Amin First Nation Treaty Settlement Lands. In fact this is true of much of the SCT north of Powell Lake, from around Malaspina Road to the end of Scout Mountain Trail. PRPAWS has worked hard to build and maintain a good working relationship and mutual respect with Tla'Amin First Nation. This land has a long history with the First Nations, and Eagle hopes that in the future there will be a way for the trail to help visitors, as well as Powell River area residents, to better appreciate and understand the ways and traditions of Aboriginal Peoples in this area.

Chief Councillor and forestry manager Clint Williams says the working relationship Tla'Amin Timber Products has with PRPAWS is a good one.

"We have no problems with the trail being there, but we want to make sure that if we need to work a certain area, say for logging, that we can." The BOMB Squad, PRPAWS and Tla'Amin Timber Products have already

Troll Bridge…"seems such an appropriate place for trolls to be."

(left) There is plenty of green on the Sliammon Lakes Trail; (above) the Shangri-La shelter, built by the BOMB Squad, with help from PRPAWS and Tla'Amin Timber Products; (right) A beautiful view of Big Sliammon Lake from this trail.

Salal *(Gaultheria shallon)*

Salal is one of the most dominant forest understory shrubs in the British Columbia coastal forest area. It grows from sea level to mid elevations, and though it may grow sparsely, at times it forms a dense barrier that is almost impossible to penetrate.

Its pinkish flowers show up in early-to-mid summer, followed by dark purple berries that were a major food source for BC's first peoples. Its strong, flexible branches and stems are resilient in heavy snow; they bend, rather than break, and are often collected for sale as decoration in floral arrangements. Plenty of salal can be found along the Sliammon Lakes section of the Sunshine Coast Trail.

worked together successfully on the Little Sliammon Recreation Site at Shangri-La, after logging was done in that area. At the beginning of the process it was a relief, Clint says, when they realized that the groups were coming to the table with a cooperative attitude.

"We had some early meetings with PRPAWS and the BOMB Squad, and took a little bit of advice from them. The big monster fir trees that you still see standing there, they requested that those be left up…At first we weren't sure if working together was going to go too well, but we realized that they're not trying to block economic development, they're wanting to make sure that people still have recreational use of the area and we see that as a positive. It was good to work with them."

What the future holds for the trail in the treaty settlement areas is not as defined as it might be, but it assures the public reasonable access to the SCT, Eagle says.

"We negotiated a clause for inclusion in the treaty, when the treaty comes about, so that the SCT will continue to exist and thrive. In fact these considerations have already been given, with trail buffers left in areas where logging has already been done."

A Lakeshore Hike

A number of features along the Sliammon Lakes Trail make this section special. There are several scenic lake views to behold. First you will come upon Thethyeth Lake, then Big Sliammon Lake, and finally Little Sliammon Lake. At various points on the trail, you will find yourself walking along the lakeshore, making for a peaceful amble that encourages lots of stops to sit and enjoy the view.

At the south end of Little Sliammon Lake there is a recreation site and a shelter named Shangri-La that was built by the BOMB Squad in 2008, with support from PRPAWS and Tla'Amin Timber Products. It replaced a dilapidated shelter of the same name that had been built some decades earlier, along with the original trail section from Wildwood to Little Sliammon Lake, by Wildwood residents.

A Bird's Eye View

The climb to the top of Scout Mountain in the next trail section is worth the effort. Once you reach the summit you will be able to see Powell Lake, Westview and Wildwood, and the ocean beyond. On a warm, sunny day you can hardly think of a better place in the world to be. If you are doing the through-hike, make the extra ascent to the very peak; the view will reward.

Starting in Wildwood and ending at Powell Lake, the Scout Mountain Trail touches on two areas with interesting local history. *Powell River's First 50 Years* describes the development of Wildwood, and where the settlement got its name:

Wildwood's real development started in 1914, when the Government divided the area into homesteads of 40 to 60 acres.

The applicants for those homesteads were a hardy and determined lot who waited in line on the Vancouver courthouse steps for 40 days and 40 nights. The "first come-first served" maxim held true, for the first in line had his choice of the pre-emptions, 13 in Wildwood and 14 in Westview, and there were 40 applicants for the 27 parcels of land…

At that time, to obtain a Crown Grant for a pre-emption, it was necessary to clear five acres, do improvements to the value of $10, for each acre in the pre-emption, and the homesteader, or a relative, must sleep on the property for ten months of the year, for five years.

The old timers, reminiscing, all agree it was a lot of hard work getting established in their new homes, but they all chuckle when they remember, and it sounds now like a lot of fun.

Fighting their way through fallen trees, sometimes three and four deep, stumps, second growth and underbrush, to find their land, they could have thought of no more appropriate name than Wildwood.

(left) The Marathon Shuffle is an annual event that attracts both walkers and runners; (right) You get a great view of Powell River from the top of Scout Mountain.

The Powell Lake Shingle Mill

The Shingle Mill Pub & Bistro is located at the south end of Scout Mountain Trail. This is a popular place for hikers to recover from the steep ascent and descent, especially after the annual Marathon Shuffle. The restaurant is located in the vicinity of one of Powell River's historic sites, an actual working shingle mill that was built around 1915 by Brooks-Bidlake.

Because of the shingle mill's relative isolation, a small settlement was established on the same site, and by 1928 there were about 50 houses, a laundry and some small businesses there as well. The shingle mill was bought by Howard Jamieson in the 1920s and it became known as the Powell Lake Shingle Mill.

(left) The Powell Lake Shingle Mill and the settlement that grew up around it was a thriving community for several decades; (above) Fire was a very real hazard that plagued the shinglemill over its lifespan. ~ photos by Maud Lane, courtesy of the Powell River Historical Museum & Archives Association.

The shingle mill and its adjoining settlement were plagued by a series of fires. In 1928 the laundry was destroyed by fire; in 1930 it was Jamieson's house; 1931 saw the burning of the sawmill itself; in 1945 another fire damaged some expensive equipment at the mill; in 1950 fire struck the shingle mill structure again. Finally, in 1951, the sawmill and planer were razed and Jamieson sold the remains to the Olsen Creek Logging Company. The property changed hands again two years later when the Powell River Company bought it in 1953. At that point most of the remaining residents had moved out and the houses were torn down for lumber. Today a marina and the pub stand as a reminder of this once-thriving settlement.

*Historical information according to articles in the Powell River News.

49

Over the Saddle
Powell River Bridge to Fiddlehead Farm

¤ Mowat Bay Trail
¤ Tony's Trail
¤ Lost Lake Trail
¤ Inland Lake Trail
¤ Confederation Lake Trail
¤ Fiddlehead Trail

In the Heart of the City

The trail sections from the Powell River Bridge to Inland Lake are some of the most easily accessed along the Sunshine Coast Trail. Located in the heart of Powell River, many of them run along areas of local historical significance.

The Mowat Bay Trail starts just after the Powell River Bridge. A lovely, short walk, it makes its way around part of the southern shore of Powell Lake, along the base of Valentine Mountain, and ends up at Mowat Bay back on Powell Lake. It's an easy way for anyone to experience at least part of the SCT, but you might want to take the opportunity to do this section soon as there is logging planned in the area by Island Timberlands Limited Partnership (ITLP), who owns that property.

On behalf of PRPAWS Eagle has been talking to ITLP for several years about the upcoming harvest. Initial talks with CEO Darshan Sihota secured an assurance that hikers would be able to continue to traverse the land, even if it is developed as a residential area sometime in the future.

"Recently ITLP advised me that they would start looking at logging this property in the fall of 2011," Eagle says. "As a result PRPAWS may have to relocate the trail within that property so it's more out of the way. However ITLP decides to deal with the issue, we will try the best we can to look after recreation and tourism interests."

Because of the ever-changing nature of as-yet unprotected stretches of trail, before starting a long trek it is always best to refer to the official SCT website, www.sunshinecoast-trail.com, for recent updates of trail conditions and information about areas that are affected by logging.

(left) Powell Lake has a lonely, ethereal beauty on cloudy days; (right, inset) View of the Shingle Mill Pub & Bistro from the Mowat Bay Trail; (far right) Another view from this pretty trail, in the heart of Powell River.

A Lake with a Story

At more than 51 kilometres in length and 416 metres at its deepest point, Powell Lake is sizeable by anyone's standards. It has over 450 kilometres of scenic shoreline, some of which contains sections of the SCT. For the past century Powell Lake has been a favourite playground for Powell Riverites wanting to get away from town. It also has a working history, as a log highway for trees that were felled "up the lake," and its shores have been home to at least two shingle mills.

Powell Lake and its surrounding areas have sheltered some interesting characters over the years, including the mysterious Robert Bonner "Billie Goat" Smith, who settled near the head of the lake at Jim Brown Creek around 1906. Billie Goat, who was from the United States, went into hiding because of a sordid past, which is rumoured to have included desertion, a bank robbery, a murder, or all three! Nevertheless, the man spent most of his life living independently off the land in near-isolation, and has provided generations since with fodder for imaginations gone wild. (Find out more at the Powell River Historical Museum & Archives).

In the Bay

The Mowat Bay Trail comes out at the park at Mowat Bay on property that once belonged to a colourful local couple by the names of Andy and Clarabelle Anderson. Andy, who was born in Sweden and raised in the United States, was given the nickname "Bull of the Woods," which speaks to the fact that he was reputedly hardworking and tough as nails right up until he died at the age of 89. Clarabelle (also known as Clara) was reported to have been just as hardy. For 28 years the Andersons owned and operated a sawmill and planing mill on land that they leased from

Salmonberry *(Rubus spectabilis)*

Salmonberries belong to the genus *Rubus*, of the rose family, and are native to the west coast of North America. An early bloomer in this area, their bright pink flowers are first to appear, followed by berries that range in colour from yellow to orange to red. Depending on ripeness and where they are growing, salmonberries can be somewhat tart to the tastebuds. They can be eaten raw, or processed into jam, jelly or wine. They were traditionally eaten by First Nations people with salmon, or mixed with oolichan grease (made from the oolichan fish) or salmon roe.

the Powell River Company at Anderson Bay on Powell Lake. When that lease was cancelled they moved the equipment to a 6.5-hectare property at Mowat Bay where they had lived since 1960. Despite the fact that there had been a sawmill at that location around 1915-1920, the municipality wouldn't allow them to operate there, so Anderson's Mill remained quiet until the late 1980s when it was moved to the Heritage Village Museum in Burnaby to be used as a historical display.

An excerpt from a story about Andy's life, which was published in the *Powell River News* on December 12, 1977 (and can be found in *Boats, Bucksaws and Blisters* by Bill Thompson), gives a hint of his character:

A close friend of Andy's, who had hunted and fished with him for 20 years said he was a "tough old boy." He worked on his booms on the lake, salvaging logs, until his heart made him quit three years ago [aged 86]…[One] time, he was going to go out on the booms. He got himself into the boat and fell out, and hung onto the logs for a couple of hours before somebody found him. This was in September, two years ago [aged 87]. All he could say when he got out of the water was 'I'm cold as a toad.' He was in the hospital over night and out again the next day.

Travelling Through to Tony's Trail

Today Mowat Bay is a popular swimming spot that boasts a park, a nice swimming beach, and a nearby boat launch. Originally, SCT hikers could walk around the bay and onto Tony's Trail, but in recent years the beginning of the trail has been rerouted due to a conflict between the municipality and a private landowner.

"This interrupts the SCT from being a trail that travels virtually exclusively through wooded or natural areas," Eagle says. "There's a stretch of trail along the eastern bayshore that has been used by the public for decades where the trail goes into and out of some wooded private property. The landowner tried to reach a deal with the city council at the time – six or seven years ago – to establish a trail corridor. They couldn't reach an agreement, and so the landowner said nobody was allowed to go along there anymore. But kids always go along the trail and jump off the rocks, which are on Crown land. If we could get to this section we could build steps onto the higher level and hook into the rest of the SCT. So that's the issue. We are hoping to revisit this matter with the new owner and council. Perhaps some kind of accommodation can be found in the future."

Until that time hikers must walk through the streets to get past the gravel pit in Cranberry, and an access trail to Tony's Trail up on Gallagher Hill (for details see Eagle's guidebook, visit the Powell River Visitor's Bureau, or check www.sunshinecoast-trail.com).

With the exception of the Gallagher Hill Connector, which was built by PRPAWS around 2003, Tony's Trail was built by local hiker and renowned outdoorsman Tony Mathews. An original member of the BOMB Squad, Tony built this trail from Mowat Bay, where he lived, to Haywire Bay. "Essentially I think it was so that he could go fishing," chuckles friend and fellow BOMB Squad founder, Roy Hewitt.

The trail now starts out on the bluffs above Mowat Bay, and offers some great views of the area, before it slopes down to and follows the lakeshore north to Haywire Bay. There are some magnificent mossy trees to be seen along the way. A great place to stop is at Tony's Point, where you can see a BOMB Squad memorial to Tony Mathews and enjoy a refreshing swim on a hot day. At the end of the trail you will pop out at Haywire Bay Regional Park, a popular summer vacation spot. In 2012 a large facility for school district outdoor education programs and people with disabilities will be opening there.

(inset) A plaque commemorating Tony Mathews at Tony's Point; (right) Beautiful, mossy trees can be found along Tony's Trail.

55

Finding Peace at Lost Lake

Walking the Lost Lake trail section makes you feel like everything around you is pulsing with life. From the mossy trees to the expansive fern fields, all is green, lush, and alive. It is the perfect place to do a little Forest Bathing, a common practice in Japan, known as *Shinrin-yoku*.

It doesn't take a scientist to figure out that taking a walk in the woods is good for the heart (in more ways than one). Most people find spending time in nature relaxing and rejuvenating, but the Japanese have taken things one step further. In 1982 the Forest Agency of Japan formally recognized Forest Bathing as a relaxation and stress management technique. It's more than the sight of the trees and nature that provides benefit, they say. It's the smells – specifically the phytoncides, or airborne chemicals emitted by plants to protect them from rotting and insects.

According to the article, "The Claim: Exposure to Plants and Parks Can Boost Immunity" in *The New York Times* (July 5, 2010), "In a series of studies, scientists found that when people swap their concrete confines for a few hours in more natural surroundings — forests, parks and other places with plenty of trees — they experience increased immune function." Stressed? Maybe it's time to get out on the SCT!

(left) A land of green in the Lost Lake Trail; (right) Looking out from Haywire Bluffs.

Old Man's Beard *(Usnea)*

The temperate rainforests in this area are so magical in part because of the incredible mosses and lichens that grow on the rocks, trees – seemingly everywhere – in every shade of green imaginable. *Usnea* is the scientific name for several species of lichen in the family *Parmeliaceae* that grow hanging from tree branches, resembling grey or greenish hair. It is also known commonly as Old Man's Beard. *Usnea* grows all over the world and certain varieties have been used medicinally for centuries. Most species contain Usnic acid, which has antibiotic and antifungal properties; consequently it was used by First Nations people as a compress for wounds to prevent infection and gangrene. Of course its structure also lent itself to this application.

Around the Loop and Up the Bluffs

The Lost Lake Trail connects Haywire Bay on Powell Lake with Lost and Inland lakes. This trail was built in the late '90s, and around 2005 PRPAWS added a 20-minute ascent through old growth up to Haywire Bluffs. From the bluffs you get a spectacular view of Powell Lake and the Shingle Mill Pub & Bistro, the mainland, and the ocean beyond. Despite the fact that it's not on the main SCT through-route, it's worth the time and energy it takes to get there. The hike up to the bluffs also makes a nice day trip, with a great view to accompany your bagged lunch.

Forget not that the earth delights to feel your bare feet and the winds long to play with your hair. ~ Kahlil Gibran

A Park for All

A well-loved local recreation area, Inland Lake, also known as Loon Lake, is a hop, skip and a jump from the centre of town. The trail that circumnavigates the lake acts as a SCT connector, linking Lost Lake Trail with Confederation Lake Trail.

Inland Lake Provincial Park, which is 2,763 hectares in size, was established in 1997, at the same time that PRPAWS negotiated Malaspina Provincial Park as part of the province's Protected Area Strategy initiative. Although PRPAWS had hoped for a much larger area of protected space, which they entitled "Pinko Park" because they drew the first outline of it over their map with a pink highlighter, it wasn't to be.

Some of the land PRPAWS had targeted became provincial park, and some of it received protected status, which means that it has special recreation considerations, and the maximum cutblock size can be no larger than 2 hectares.

Before Inland Lake became a provincial park, it was contained within a Forest Service Recreation Area, a 100-metre-wide riparian zone that surrounded the lake. A 13-kilometre trail that circles the lake was constructed by the Model Community Society and boasts wheelchair access all the way around. Besides walking and running, mountain biking, camping, swimming, fishing and canoeing are all activities that people enjoy at the park. There are several lovely boardwalks to be found along the trail, and many inhabitants like birds, frogs, toads and snakes, as well as a number of plant species to observe and enjoy.

Since 1995 the Loon Lake Race has been a popular local event that raises money for charity. Participants walk or run 13 kilometres around the lake, or do a total of 7 kilometres out to Anthony Island and back. As the official race website proclaims: "Where else in coastal BC can you run on 13+ kilometres of wide manicured trail around a lake without even a bump? The biggest single gain of elevation — The Hill — is about 8 to 10 vertical feet!" Anyone who is hiking the whole SCT will especially appreciate this rare flat area.

A Trail Challenge

You will realize your break is over as soon as you start the steep climb to Confederation Lake. But between gasps, take time to appreciate the fact that the Confederation Lake Trail was at one time a good deal worse.

Before Scott had started doing much hiking locally – before he had even met Eagle – he learned about the trail to Confederation Lake.

"Margot and I used to go to California to go hiking on the Pacific Coast Trail and in the Sierras. At one point we said, 'Why are we travelling a thousand miles to go hiking when there have got to be places to hike here?' So we started looking into what there was. We realized that there were only seven or eight trails that were marked and official, and at one point someone told us about Confederation Lake.

The Confederation Lake and Fiddlehead trails were built by Peter Scheiber, who, along with his wife Linda, owned Fiddlehead Farm. According to Linda he built them because he wanted to be able to hike into Powell River in emergency situations.

The Confederation Lake Trail is a brutal climb, and it's often littered with tree limbs and debris, Margot says. "It goes through territory that the wind whistles through and every single year you've got blowdown – and the blowdown is huge! Some people we knew used to go up there to go fishing, and they called it Draggin' Ass Lake – because you're draggin' your ass all the way up there!"

Scott remembers his first encounters with the trail, and when he and Eagle started working to improve it. "Margot and I hiked up there a couple of

(left) Confederation Lake Trail boasts some spectacular old growth sections; (inset) Confederation Lake; (right) Misty days are quiet and ghostly along this trail.

times, and I can remember saying to myself, 'I cannot imagine the crazy people who carried chainsaws up here and actually cleared this trail.' Within about five years of that statement, I was one of them – and I was not only carrying one chainsaw, I carried two chainsaws and two packs up to Confederation Lake one time!" He laughs. "I thought, 'This is karma!' I had a crew at one point to put in some of the switchbacks there, but it's still an evil trail."

Peace, and Quiet?

Though it may be steep, the Confederation Lake Trail will take you through some magnificent areas of old growth. It's a stretch of trail with many moods. When the weather has been dry, it can be hot and humourless, stark and brown. However, if there has been lots of rain, it is playful – somewhat reminiscent of Fern Gully. When the mist sets in among the giants, it can be ghostly. One of the rewards for the two-to-three hour climb is peaceful Confederation Lake at the top where a cabin awaits weary hikers. This cabin was built by a local logging contractor who had a debt to pay to BC Forest Service for some unauthorized harvesting of shake blocks. It is now maintained by BC Parks. All huts and cabins along the SCT are for shared, public use. Keeping this in mind, it might be an idea to throw a pair of earplugs in your pack if you are planning an overnight stay – just in case you happen to run into Scott and Eagle. Don Krompocker and Lita Biron, long-time board members of PRPAWS, can attest to that. Scott delights in telling the story.

"Eagle and I apparently snore louder than any two people on the planet," he laughs. "One time we went up to Confederation Lake with about eight people. Me and Eagle and Lita and Don were in the cabin. There were four bunks. This is the way Don tells it: 'Here we are in the cabin and everyone's been hiking for six hours, and we're all tired, so we go to bed. It's 9 or 10 o'clock and we start to go to sleep, and within about 15 seconds Scott and

(left) The Confederation Lake Trail is lush and green when rains have been generous; (above) The cabin at Confederation Lake.

Eagle fall asleep and start snoring like freight trains! Lita looks over the bunk and goes, 'I can't believe how loud they're snoring! I don't know if I can get to sleep here!'

"This goes on for about an hour," Scott continues. "We're just snoring like pigs. Finally after about an hour and a half Don and Lita start drowsing, and they're just about getting off to sleep and all of a sudden Taz – Eagle's dog – notices a mouse in the cabin and starts barking at the top of his lungs. So Eagle gets up and puts Taz outside. Again they start to settle back down, and they're just about to drift off to sleep again, and Taz decides he doesn't like being outside and starts HOWLING! When these guys are telling the story, they say, 'We got about two hours of sleep that night between your snoring and that dog!'"

"The Farm"

Behind the cabin at Confederation Lake, the SCT continues, and turns into the Fiddlehead trail section. This trail winds through some lovely second growth and old growth forest, and some stunning viewpoints before descending to a plot of land with a fascinating history. This land, most recently known as Fiddlehead Farm, has been loved and neglected in turn; it has been tamed by humans, reclaimed by nature, tamed by humans and reclaimed by nature again. Besides Fiddlehead Farm, it has been known as Powell Lake Farm and "The Farm". It has been a homestead, a market farm, a hippie commune, an alternative school, and a healing gathering place.

This 32-hectare piece of land sits almost 20 kilometres up Powell Lake, and a couple of kilometres inland. Until the surrounding areas were logged for the second time in the early 2000s, Powell Lake was the easiest way to access the property. Now it is accessible via logging road, and, of course, the SCT (which in part follows the trail that was originally built by Peter Scheiber).

The earliest settlers on this land were Italians by the names of Giuseppe Gagliardi, who was known as "Little Joe," and his uncle Dominico Diana. Prior to 1914, Little Joe took half a pre-emption (which consisted of the 32-hectare plot) and Dominico came to help work the farm once the land was cleared. In the 1920s and '30s Little Joe and Dominico had an impressive market garden, growing everything from eggplants to potatoes. They also raised goats, and later sheep. During harvest season they made a weekly trip into Powell River to sell their goods.

When Little Joe died he willed the property to Sam Spatari, a Powell River Company tailor. For many years the farm stood vacant, waiting for its next human inhabitants.

They didn't come until the early 1970s, and "they" were a group of young Americans who were disenchanted with the Vietnam War and society in general. These searchers were looking for something more; somewhere where things made sense. They found it at the farm at Powell Lake. Writer Mark Vonnegut was one of the group.

Vomit Vista

Sometimes you would be surprised at how places get their names...

"The trail from Confederation to Fiddlehead was relatively new at the time this spot was named. There were some places where if you just cut down a couple of trees you would get a better view – mind you they were awful sickly trees. One time Eagle and I were working near Confederation Lake. Eagle wasn't feeling particularly well. 'So,' he said, 'you are going to have to cut those trees down and I will just lie here and throw up. I know! We'll call it Vomit Vista.'" ~ Scott Glaspey

On renaming Powell Lake Farm:

"Because we're Quakers and pacifists my husband didn't like the idea of the farm being named after a military man so we changed it to Fiddlehead because in the spring we had so many fiddlehead ferns coming up everywhere." ~ Linda Scheiber

In his engaging book, *The Eden Express*, Mark describes his first encounter with the farm:

We got to the farm after tromping a mile and a half on a soggy, misty, overgrown trail. The place was more beautiful than our wildest dreams. Lush blackberries ripening, apple trees with green fruit. Several acres of field still clear. A stream ran right by the old house. Mountains on all sides. If there was any hesitation in my mind I missed it...We walked around for a couple of hours uncovering more and more marvelous things. There were little trout in the stream, old harnesses and hardware in a collapsed shed, a wine cellar with old casks, lots of garter snakes and friendly toads...I guess deep down inside I had never really believed it was going to happen; that we would really find something, let alone something so perfect, so beautiful, so cheap. I breathed huge sighs of relief. Home at last.

Mark and a few friends bought Powell Lake Farm for $12,000, and established a small hippie commune there. They added to the existing house (a third floor so that "the damned thing looked like a pterodactyl learning to fly"), and welcomed like-minded travellers looking for a place to stay. It lasted but a few years, ending shortly after Mark was forced to leave because of mental health issues that were aggravated by the isolation of the farm. His journey into and back from madness is the subject of *The Eden Express*. Though the farm was unoccupied once again, that didn't last long. One of the group who had lived at the commune was also a teacher at an alternate school in Vancouver called Total Education, and he recommended the farm as a perfect rural sub-location for the school. Peter and Linda Scheiber, two Quaker teachers, agreed to run the Total Education program for a year, at the commune site. Having spent part of their lives living in a remote BC setting, they fell in love with the place, and ended up purchasing it, continuing the outdoor education program, and an alternative wilderness school for some time.

"In between milking the goats and building a pottery kiln, the kids down here on the farm are learning *Twelfth Night*," reported an article in the November 26, 1976 issue of the *Vancouver Sun*. "And it's quite likely the

(left) Fiddlehead Farm was renamed for the fiddleheads that grow so well on the property; (right) Fiddlehead Farm during its heyday. ~ photos to the right courtesy of Linda Scheiber

boys will be doing the dishes while the girls are hammering and sawing at some new cabin steps. Because that's the way things work at Powell River Farm, which must be one of the most unusual and exciting schools in the province."

Then the Scheibers' lives changed. "My husband died in 1985," Linda explains, "Our children and I needed to expand. We had animals and a big garden. We also had a place that we knew could provide unusual life experiences beyond what we had been involved with to that point. We started having international hostellers come to live on the farm, get to know the wild surroundings, and earn their way by helping with the work. Fiddlehead Farm became a destination for travellers from all over the world who wanted to live for a while, the old-fashioned Canadian, pioneer life, and to meet wild BC backcountry face-to-face."

It was a special place that appealed to people who were interested in living close to the land, learning to be somewhat self-sufficient, and tuning in to nature. After being featured in a couple of prominent magazines, including *Beautiful British Columbia* and *Westworld*, there was no further need to advertise Fiddlehead Farm.

"We were flooded with guests who wanted to come, and the farm became an eco-destination for families from Vancouver. The business grew into a combination of international travelers and young families." Besides the everyday business of running a farm they held programs for children and a variety of music and healing gathering workshops.

Over the years the Scheibers and their visitors built trails and several buildings, including a sauna/bathhouse, a dormitory, and a dining room/kitchen. But more than physical structures, they created a lifestyle that provided many people with rich and unusual, happy memories.

"I still correspond with many of the people who came there," says Linda. "We changed people's lives, particularly the young travellers looking for something different, in search of themselves. Many of them fell in love there. It was a very romantic place, and a nurturing environment to be in." All three of Peter's and Linda's children married partners they met at

Fiddlehead Farm.

Fiddlehead Farm was still in operation in the early years of the SCT's development, and during that time it was a favourite stop for through-hikers on the trail. But, the property was located in the midst of a working, second-growth forest. By 2002 the trees in the Crown lands surrounding the farm, had matured to the point where the timber licence holder (what is now Western Forest Products) wanted to log.

Linda was 65 and her children had lives away from the farm. It was time to sell. This excerpt from a story in *The Peak* newspaper from March 11, 2003 explains what happened next:

In a letter to The Peak, Liisa Hamilton, Scheiber's daughter, wrote that after the farm had been on the market for over a year and a half, [a buyer] approached her mother. "He seemed to be the first person who had a realistic business plan. He walked through the property and said that he would need to selectively log in order to recoup some of his costs and then he planned to either continue running the ecotourism business, or resell it to someone who would. The one thing that he made clear was that he intended to leave the bottom half of the property with the buildings untouched by logging to preserve the business as an asset. He also promised not to sell the farm to Weyerhaeuser under any circumstances."

Her mistake, Linda says today, was that she didn't have a written commitment that the buyer wouldn't log it or sell it to Weyerhaeuser. Shortly after the paperwork had been signed the property was logged flat, the buildings burned down, and the clear-cut was sold to Weyerhaeuser. It was a sad ending for Fiddlehead Farm, and a big loss for the SCT as well, Eagle says.

(left) A swing hanging from an apple tree is one of the only signs today of the vibrant farm that once occupied these lands; (above) Nature is once again in the process of reclaiming the former Fiddlehead Farm.

"Fiddlehead Farm was such an asset to the trail. It brought a lot of attention to what we are trying to do here. It was very disappointing when the farm was lost."

Today signs of human occupation are difficult to pick out; nature has once again claimed this land. But it's a spot that calls to something deep inside those seeking something other than the hectic pace of city life. So, who knows what its future will bring?

Tin Hats and Mountain Ranges
Fiddlehead Farm to Eagle River

¤ West Tin Hat Mountain Trail
¤ Tin Hat Mountain Trail
¤ Lewis Lake Trail
¤ March Lake Trail
¤ Elk Lake Loop Trail
¤ Walt Hill Trail
¤ Suicide Pass Trail
¤ Smokey's Blue Ridge
¤ Eagle River Trail

Climbing to a Splendid View

Once you have had the chance to look around the property that was once Fiddlehead Farm, you will forge ahead, onwards and upwards toward the peak of Tin Hat Mountain. The West Tin Hat Trail winds its way up the side of the mountain in a relatively gentle manner, and will treat you to passage through beautiful mature second-growth forest. When you reach an area of the trail that crosses numerous massive boulders, look up and down. This is an impressive ancient slide and the boulders, some the size of small houses, reach down the mountainside into the valley bottom.

Tin Hat Mountain, which was named for the metal safety helmets that were worn by early loggers, rises to an elevation of approximately 1,200 metres. Since the former Fiddlehead Farm property is not far above sea level, you have a fair bit of climbing to do. Carry on, knowing that a splendid view awaits you at the top. A cabin, that was finished in the fall of 2011, is now located close to the summit, and provides a welcome place to stop for a rest, or to spend the night.

Coming Full Circle

At one time the summit of Tin Hat Mountain was home to a fire lookout station, placed there because of the incredible 360-degree view you get from that location.

"Someone stayed up there the whole fire season," explains Rudi van Zwaaij, president of the Powell River Forestry Museum. "That was one of the main forestry lookouts for fire, so it had a manned station. The next one was on Pocahontas on Texada Island."

The appointed person stayed up at the top of the mountain from around mid-May to mid-October, while the area was free of snow. There was a metal structure with a wooden shack on top, and attendants had to report in every day on the radio phone. Once the building fell into disuse it became victim to vandals, and eventually it was removed.

(left) *The new hut atop Tin Hat Mountain; (above) The spectacular view from the hut, showing Haslam Lake, Malaspina Strait, Texada Island and Vancouver Island beyond; (below) Eagle, Scott, and Jim Stutt share a laugh while taking a building break inside the new cabin.*

When Jim Stutt first moved to Powell River more than 30 years ago, he began to learn about the history of the area while he was helping to convert a former youth centre into the building that currently houses the Powell River Historical Museum & Archives. He was working on the project with Golden Stanley, the first museum director. Golden, who grew up in the Horseshoe Valley, kept talking about Tin Hat Mountain.

"Getting to know the history of the area, I felt kind of connected to it," Jim says. "I had two young kids at the time, so my wife and I were pretty focused on the home, but I did have a desire to get out in the backcountry. I had always wanted to go up to the old building on Tin Hat, but it got destroyed, and they took it down. I distinctly remember thinking it would be great if someone rebuilt that. And now, we're doing just that! So, to me that is some big connected thing. It's funny when you have those intentions how they can come around."

Nature does not hurry, yet everything is accomplished. ~ Lao Tzu

XS-NRG

Tin Hat Mountain seems an appropriate place to mention one of the great adventures that has occurred along the Sunshine Coast Trail, mostly because it was a turning point for some of the participants. For those who have hiked the trail, and know how challenging it is, it's difficult to imagine what was going through the heads of four endurance athletes from Vancouver when they decided to run the whole trail – 180 kilometres without stopping. This epic run was made into a movie called *XS-NRG* that has brought some national attention to the SCT.

But let's back up just a bit. It's an interesting story that starts with four high-energy friends, some beer, and the Tour de France. Ean Jackson, one of the team, remembers how the idea came about:

"I didn't really know anything about the SCT," he says, "except that it was there and it sounded kind of cool. But then my buddies and I were watching the Tour de France and drinking beer one night, and we started talking about what we were going to do that year. We couldn't do Ironman or the Western States 100-mile run, because they were both full, so what were we going to do? Somebody said something about the SCT; it's a 100-miler, but no one's ever run it. And we all clued in right there. We didn't know anything about it, but we decided we were going to do it!"

The next night, assembled to watch the next leg of the famous cycling race, the idea evolved. One of them pulled out Eagle's guidebook, and they had a look through it. Ean called Eagle up to get more details, and the challenge began.

When Eagle received this phone call out of the blue, he was a little taken aback.

"Well, I had a conversation with Scott about it, and in his usual bravado he said things like, 'If they die it's their own fault!'" Eagle laughs. "I said I thought it would be really, really tough, but maybe it could be done. It was

(left) From the top of Tin Hat Mountain during the Golden Hour; right) Eagle takes a break at the boulder field on the West Tin Hat Trail.

Ean Jackson relived part of his XS-NRG run in the 2010 Marathon Shuffle.

Club Fat Ass

Club Fat Ass was founded in 2003 by Ean Jackson 10 years after he hosted the first annual New Year's Day Fat Ass 50-kilometre run in Vancouver. That event was inspired by runner Joe Oakes, who organized the very first Fat Ass event in 1979, so he could get a qualifying time for the Western States 100-Mile Endurance Run. Since then numerous events have sprung up around the world, the concept being "low-key, no frills, and low or no cost." In an attempt to help spread the word about the SCT, Club Fat Ass adopted the annual Marathon Shuffle as one of its events, which is one of the reasons it attracts a number of runners from Vancouver each year.

a long shot, but if I could marshal enough support for them to make it through, maybe that would help."

Ean recalls the phone call well. It went something like this:

Ean: Tell me a little bit about the trail, we're thinking of running it.

Eagle: Oh, you can't run it!

Ean: Well how long does it take to walk without stopping?

Eagle: It can't be done.

Ean: We're going to run it in two days!

Eagle: You can't do that, it takes us seven days and we're pretty tough up here!

The delight in Ean's voice is palpable. "We were a bunch of city boys, but we decided to do it in two days! And we asked Eagle to help us. He said, 'Well, you can't do it, but I'll think about it.'"

That summer of 2003 Ean Jackson, David Cressman and brothers Dom and Wade Repta came to Powell River to give the SCT a try. They started at Sarah Point and made it to Fiddlehead Farm, but then they got lost.

"We ran almost 100 kilometres and then we got so badly lost, we almost died," Ean says, still laughing. "It got really late, and we were a long way from where we needed to go. All our warm gear was up at Tin Hat Mountain. If it weren't for a Polish man who was on his houseboat on Powell Lake, we would have got our asses kicked. We got saved. Eagle found the road in the middle of the night. He picked us up, saved our hides. We rested in our tents for a couple of hours, then two of us decided we were going to keep on going. And we got terribly, terribly lost the second day – again!!"

After the second setback, they decided to call it a wrap, but the boys had the bug; this was a trail they wanted to conquer. Before they had even boarded the ferry at Saltery Bay they had decided to do it again, better, the following year.

In 2004 they came prepared. They brought a support crew with them, and pacers – people who could run sections with them along the way so they didn't have to spend too much energy figuring out where to go. Eagle, Scott and PRPAWS volunteers had the trail in top form. The team's goal was to get at least one of the runners to the end of the trail, without stopping. They started at 2 am in the early morning of July 3. At 16 hours and 23 minutes they had reached 81 kilometres and Fiddlehead Farm. That's where David Cressman started losing his equilibrium. He was the first runner to crack. The other three brought him up and down, over Tin Hat Mountain, to where they knew support was waiting for them. They reached the checkpoint after clocking 92 kilometres in 20 hours and 34 minutes. At that point Dom and Wade Repta couldn't imagine running another 88 kilometres. So Ean Jackson was the last runner standing. He decided to carry on, into the Smith Range as night fell.

"We were at the bottom of Tin Hat and Ean was still ready to go," Eagle remembers, "but nighttime was approaching quickly. He was quite disappointed, and he realized he would have to abandon it, unless he had someone to go with him to Elk Lake. One of the pacers – they called them the Whistler Boys – was at the Walt Hillton, an emergency shelter just before the ridge of Walt Hill. I knew if I could get Ean to Elk Lake, then the trail system was easy to follow on the inside route, and on up to Coyote Lake. We had cleared the trail a lot, but the marking then was nowhere as good as it is now. I told Ean I would get him up there, so I, and a couple of other guys, put on our headlamps and paced him up as far as Elk Lake. From there the trail followed an old road system for quite a distance; that was around midnight. While we turned around, Ean carried on and found his next pacer asleep and freezing in the Walt Hillton. They ran on through the night and made it over top of Walt Hill, down the south slope, and in the morning, with still over 40 kilometres and one huge mountain to go, they popped out at Mile 4 on Goat Main."

(right) Spring Lake is a beautiful spot that can be seen at the end of the Lewis Lake Trail.

As the other runners had recovered after a good night's sleep, they joined Ean again. They ascended the 1300-metre Mount Troubridge and began the long descent, finally reaching their goal as night set in once more. Ean ran the whole distance in 43 hours and 50 minutes, non-stop. He still holds the record as the fastest, and only, person to complete the SCT without stopping. He hopes that someone else will take on the challenge to beat his time.

"It will happen," Ean says. "It could be one of those really neat things that has a really exclusive cult following – those who want to run the SCT. People will come from all over to check it out!"

A Pilot Project

As you leave the Tin Hat Mountain section you will hike around the east side of Lewis Lake and south to Spring Lake via the Lewis Lake Trail. By hiking this section you can see the effects a treed buffer has on a trail, as well as the effects of no buffer at all. The beginning of the Lewis Lake section enjoys a 100-metre-wide reserve zone that was established when that area was logged, as per the regulations and objectives of the Stillwater Timberlands Pilot Project, enacted by the government in 2001. However, since that time, Weyerhaeuser, the company that signed off on the project, has changed hands – first to Cascadia, and soon after to Western Forest Products (WFP).

As the companies changed hands, the pilot project was terminated. This turn of events was frustrating and discouraging, Eagle says. A lot of time was spent by PRPAWS and many other community stakeholders over a period of several years providing input to develop the project, and to negotiate community values such as adequate trail buffers. But the mandatory guidelines that resulted were only followed for six years, and then discontinued. A new stewardship plan replaced the Stillwater Timberlands Pilot Project.

"Mandatory project trail buffer objectives have become voluntary, and this has resulted, generally, in narrower treed buffers, or none at all in some instances," Eagle says. When windfirming (to stop trees from being so

(left) A moss-covered cedar tree; (above) From the March Lake trail section.

vulnerable to wind) is carried out, it makes it easier to maintain the trail because there are fewer blowdowns. Without precautionary windfirming, however, excessive blowdowns may make trail sections difficult to navigate, especially if volunteers have not had time to do maintenance after a storm.

Today PRPAWS negotiates to protect the SCT on a cutblock-by-cutblock basis, and in terms of the section of the trail that runs through WFP's Tree Farm Licence, site-specific planning works best, says Operations Planner Stuart Glen. He is the one who does a field walk with Eagle whenever WFP starts to look at harvesting an area the trail runs through.

"Inevitably there are going to be times when harvesting is somewhere along the trail since it goes through the working forest," he says. "We have included the SCT in our Canadian Standards Association Sustainable Forest Management Plan. I think we've learned that when you get down to the detail of the management of a trail it really does become site specific."

Managing things site specifically makes it possible to achieve the best results, considering all the different factors WFP has to consider, Stuart continues. He adds that a buffer is not always realistic, or best for a given site from a forestry perspective. "We manage for the trail the best we can, while at the same time facilitating the harvesting of areas along the trail."

79

Ghost Camp

Towards the end of the Lewis Lake Trail you will reach Spring Lake and the trail turns into an old railroad grade. Though the area is grown over and moss-covered today, 90 years ago it was the site of a thriving logging camp that housed about 300 people. According to an interview with Bob Gela Jr., as quoted in *Once Upon A Stump* by Bill Thompson, the Spring Lake camp was where trainloads of timber were made up from wood that was brought down from Lewis Lake and the surrounding areas. In 1928 a devastating fire decimated the camp and surrounding forest lands, and the camp was never re-established in that location. If you are observant, evidence of the camp can still be seen. A steam donkey kettle cap sticks out of the lake, and rusty artefacts like wheelbarrows, the odd saw blade, bed springs, sinks, a woodstove, and old logging cable litter the areas around the trail.

(left, top) An old logging cable peeks out from the ground where it lies buried in the past; (left, middle) Massive stumps left by loggers almost a century ago hint of the forest of giants that once lived here; (left, bottom) Rusty remains serve as reminders of the vibrant logging camp that thrived in this area in the early 20th Century; (far right) Spring Lake Logging Camp ca. 1924 ~ photo courtesy of the Powell River Forestry Museum.

Annual Allowable Cut

Each year logging companies are required to cut a five-year average of an Annual Allowable Cut (AAC), which is a volume of trees determined by the companies, and approved (or altered) by the chief forester of British Columbia. The AAC is based on a number of factors, including availability, growth rates and social values. Though there is some flexibility from year-to-year which allows for fluctuations in the market, if a logging company does not fill their required AAC over any given five-year period, it risks losing that portion of the cut it has been allotted for harvesting, but which it has not harvested. This is because government wants to ensure it has a steady income from the stumpage payments it receives from the logging companies. As a result, when members of the public are lobbying to protect forests, it's not only the logging companies they need to address, but also the government, which controls the bigger picture.

Marching into the Swamps of Doom

The March Lake Trail contains two extraordinary stands of old growth trees – one of Western redcedar, and the other of Douglas fir. But making a trail that would meander through these features was no simple task. Scott and Eagle groan when they remember the experience of building the March Lake Trail through what they refer to as the *Swamps of Doom*.

"We were bushwhacking south on what ended up being the March Lake trail section," Eagle says. "We had gotten as far as the old growth cedar patch, and the weather turned for the worse. So we made camp there, and then it really started to howl." As they were getting set up Eagle fed his dog, Taz. As per normal he opened the bag of food, allowing Taz to take what he needed. However, that night Taz was particularly hungry. "We didn't pay much attention because we were trying to get a fire going, and to survive ourselves. The next time I looked over there was nothing left! He had gobbled up probably five days' worth of food." The next day it was still raining and after reluctantly sharing their human food with Taz, they started out, looking for the most direct route to the next highlight they had identified: a patch of old growth Douglas fir.

"Everything was wet – we were wet and we were miserable. Wherever we went we ran into swamp. Using our compasses did not work. The needles just kept flipping around and around! There was no way of telling what was up and what was down, or which way to go. I think we were probably stuck for two days trying to figure out a way to put a trail through. Eventually we found it, but it was tortuous; we were just snaking along, trying to stay on ground that was above water level. It was hard to find, but eventually we found it and crossed over Alaska Pine Road and headed on down to the next feature which was the old growth Douglas fir."

Ambling along the March Lake Trail you will surely agree it was worth the effort. Happening upon these two imposing and majestic stands, which are now established as Old Growth Management Areas, is truly an enchanting experience. The old growth fir patch is the only place along the SCT where there are so many huge, ancient trees assembled together.

(left) Sunlight plays with mist on the March Lake Trail; (right) Old growth fir patch.

For in the true nature of things, if we rightly consider, every green tree is far more glorious than if it were made of gold and silver. ~ Martin Luther

Up, Up, and Away

Heading up the March Lake and Elk Lake trails you will start to ascend into the Smith Mountain Range. After a steep hike up to Elk Lake you will appreciate the sight of one of the SCT's new huts, built by PRPAWS and ATV club members. Because Elk Lake is accessible only by walking or ATV (All Terrain Vehicle), the help of local ATV club members was key in getting this hut built in such a timely manner. On a hot day you may be grateful for the opportunity to jump into the lake to cool off. A swimming dock, built at the same time as the hut, makes this a most pleasing experience. If you have the chance to stay overnight, be sure to stay up for the late show, featuring a brilliant spectacle of stars.

Once you have reached Elk Lake, you can take either the inside or outside leg of the loop trail if you are through-hiking to the Walt Hill Trail. Wild blueberries and yellow cedar are some of the dominant species you will see in this area. The scenic outside loop, where you will enjoy fantastic views of the Horseshoe Valley and occasional peeks at the Knucklehead Mountains, is the better choice.

With high elevations come cooler temperatures, and snow in the chilly months. The Smith Range, encompassing the sections of the SCT from Elk Lake Loop through to Suicide Pass Trail, is perfect for those who pine for the white stuff. With the hut now located at Elk Lake, and another planned for the top of Walt Hill (2012), this area will be more usable than ever before as a winter activity destination.

(left) Elk Lake Hut under the stars; (right) OGMAs, like this one on the Confederation Lake Trail, can be found all along the Sunshine Coast Trail.

Old Growth Management Areas

Old Growth Management Areas (OG-MAs) are identified based on a variety of criteria and features, including individual forest-stand attributes, high-value wildlife habitat, patch size, forest-interior habitat, spatial distribution across the landscape, and connectivity (eg. low-to-high elevation connections, or linkages between watersheds). Established in the late 1990s, OGMA is a designation given by the province, which is meant to protect the land and forests within from logging. All Crown land is divided into landscape units, which are usually based on vast watersheds. Within most of these the province has identified and approved amounts of land base to be dedicated to OGMAs.

"OGMAs are intended to be left alone," says Russell Brewer, Practices Forester with British Columbia Timber Sales (BCTS). "But they can be amended. If they are being amended, there has to be equivalent or better replacement habitat area."

BCTS is working with PRPAWS to protect parts of the Sunshine Coast Trail that run through land BCTS is responsible for by rerouting the trail into OGMAs, where it is feasible. This has occurred in the Fairview Bay section where logging altered the location of the trail in 2011. The same thing has been done with another section of the trail located in Western Forest Products' Tree Farm Licence.

What it Takes to Build a Trail

For those who have never built a trail, it may be difficult to imagine what that actually means. How do you get started? Do you just head out into the bush and start hacking? How do you figure out the best way to go?

To the trail-building novice the process may look haphazard, but building a good trail takes some experience, Scott says, and there is method to the madness. "After a while you start to look at the topography of the land and you realize that if you want to go from A to B, there is a particularly good way of doing it. In some cases you have to go from A to B, so then you are looking for the best, or only, way of doing it. There is something about building trails that just hooks people. I remember reading about a man from Oregon, a postmaster. He was supposed to deliver mail from one side of a mountain to the other and there was no road. So he made a road by hand, for wagons – 20 miles! I remember saying, 'This guy should be in our club!'"

Building trail is rewarding, Don Krompocker adds. "Often after we've hacked a new section of trail, Scott will look at it and say, 'People are going to think it was always like this!' But they had to see it beforehand. When you go back and look at what you have done in a day, you realize how much you have accomplished."

To many people it becomes an obsession, Scott continues. "I don't even know if I can tell you why I'm addicted to it, but there's no one involved in this that isn't obsessive." The most hardcore have the chance to earn a Wombat Badge. Wombats are Australian marsupials; Scott describes them as giant guinea pigs. They grow to about 1-metre high, and weigh 20 to 35 kilograms.

"Wombats are known more than anything for their stubbornness. Apparently if you build a fence across a wombat's normal path, they will lean on that fence for an eternity, until the fence falls over. They just won't give up! Anybody who moves dirt with a mattock – and there are only about five of us – they automatically get a Wombat Badge."

THE ABCs of Trailbuilding

How does a trail end up being where it is? That's a question many people wonder, Eagle says.

"I guess it starts with an idea, and the idea is to connect point A with point B, linking two features. In between we look for a route that is gentle, and has as little elevation change as possible. The country is very hilly here and you do have to make ups and downs. So when the side hills are steep we build switchbacks into them. You have to look at maps and see what's between point A and point B. Are there streams or lakes that constrain your movement? Are there any mountain walls that would prevent you from going there? Is it too steep? Is it just right? Are there any watercourses you can follow? Then you look at forest cover maps. People in the forest industry were kind enough to share that information with us as we built the Sunshine Coast Trail, so we could find out where the old growth was. If there was old growth anywhere, we would look for a way to go up to that. We just kept making distances between points shorter and shorter, finding points of interest or a good base route.

"Once you know you want to go in a general direction and that there are no physical circumstances that would prevent you from doing so, then you check out aerial photos for bluffs and things of that nature. Bluffs mean being able to see – getting some sunlight, not having to build as much, or to clean as much because it is more open – so we would always look for a bluff for those reasons. Also it's nice to have a view rather than being under forest cover all the time. Then we would take a kilometre or two at a time, and go back and forth, or stumble back and forth is more like it! And see if there is good footing underneath. It doesn't matter if you have a wall of apparently impenetrable vegetation, if you know that here you have flat surface and that there is flat surface on the other side, you blow through the log jam, or whatever is in your way, and you have a good trail then."

(left) Though the trail has been built there is still constant maintenance and upgrading to be done. Scott, Jim and Terry Roberts build a new set of stairs on the Fairview Bay Trail; (right, inset) Scott and Don on an early years work party ~ Eagle Walz photo; (right) Eagle cuts a fallen tree off the West Tin Hat Trail.

An Easier Way

Walt Hill is one of the most inaccessible parts of the SCT, in terms of entry and exit points. As you are huffing and puffing your way up the hill, thinking to yourself, 'There must be an easier way,' be assured, there could have been.

"We could have gone an easier way to get south to Lois Lake or Eagle River from Coyote Lake," Eagle says. "We could have avoided going over Walt Hill." But the trail was not built to be easy, short and direct; it was built to highlight features that make up the backcountry around Powell River.

Also, in order to protect the trail as much as possible, one of the things Eagle and Scott considered when they were initially mapping the trail out was locations that would be less likely to compete with the interests of logging companies.

"There were already constraints on logging in certain areas – like scrawny old growth on the tops of ridges," Eagle says. "The old growth on top of a 1200-metre-high ridge, like the one along the ridge of Walt Hill, is certainly less imposing than one that's of the same age at 500-metres or 300-metres elevation. But the old growth along this stretch is still beautiful, a good example of yellow cedar old growth at that elevation." The ridge along the top of Walt Hill is now protected within an OGMA.

The Walt Hill Trail provides impressive views of the Horseshoe Valley, Lois Lake, and all the lakes of the canoe route, as well as the mountain ridges beyond. Until the cabin is built, hikers can take refuge in the "Walt Hillton," an old repeater station that was once used for controlling logging traffic. There still is a functioning repeater station at the summit of Walt Hill, but you can't see it from the trail.

(left) This view from Walt Hill shows Lois Lake and the Tantalus Range in Sechelt in the far distance; (above) An aerial view of the Walt Hillton.

Finding Suicide Pass

Suicide Pass is a trail connection that Scott describes as a happy accident. In the foreword to *The Sunshine Coast Trail* guidebook, he writes about how he and Don found this trail – completely by chance as they were thrashing around in the woods one day:

In 1995, Don Krompocker and I were out looking for a trail connection in the Smith Range. After a couple of hours, we found ourselves on a steep hillside and discovered we were headed completely in the wrong direction. In typical calm fashion Don announced, "That's it, we're lost – we're going to die." We stumbled back on our flagged line and had lunch with a bottle of red wine. After eating, we made one of those bad decisions that turned out beautifully. We wandered off in a different direction downhill. Within 15 minutes we found an old overgrown railway grade, followed it, and popped out of the bush exactly where we had wanted to come out. By pure fluke we had extended the SCT by two more kilometres.

The spring of Suicide Creek, which drains down into Lang Creek in the Duck Lake area, is located in Suicide Pass. It is a pretty section of trail with some old growth along the riparian area of the creek. Much of the trail currently follows an historic logging railroad grade, but PRPAWS may relocate the trail into the OGMA along the creek, which would run parallel to the current trail, since WFP has plans to log over the former railroad grade in the future.

Fertile Land

Smokey's Blue Ridge Trail traverses some of the best growing land along the coast. A combination of rich soil, plenty of water and southern exposure means that trees grow quickly here, and a 100-year-old tree can easily reach 1-metre in diameter, and sometimes even more.

This trail – and the Smith Mountain Range – is named after Ernest Alvia "Smokey" Smith, a BC resident and recipient of the Victoria Cross. Smokey was a character known to challenge authority, which is perhaps why in his early military career he was promoted to corporal nine times, and each time demoted back to private (prior to 1944). A citation from the *London Gazette* (December 20, 1944) tells the story of the night that Smokey earned the prestigious Victoria Cross.

Red Huckleberry *(Vaccinium parvifolium)*

"Huckleberry" is the common name for several plants in the *Ericaceae* family, in two closely related genera: *Vaccinium* and *Gaylussacia*, which also includes blueberries and cranberries. Although some of the darker huckleberries look like blueberries, they are not the same plant, and have quite a different taste. Huckleberries range in colour from bright red to dark purple and blue, ripen in mid-to-late summer, and are enjoyed by many mammals, including bears and humans. They can be eaten raw, or used to make jams, preserves, pies and cobblers. Red huckleberries grow primarily in the western part of North America, preferring the slightly acidic soils in the coastal regions.

In Italy on the night of 21st-22nd October 1944, a Canadian Infantry Brigade was ordered to establish a bridgehead across the Savio River. The Seaforth Highlanders of Canada were selected as the spearhead of the attack, and in weather most unfavourable to the operation they crossed the river and captured their objective in spite of strong opposition from the enemy.

Torrential rain had caused the Savio River to rise six feet in five hours, and as the soft vertical banks made it impossible to bridge the river no tanks or anti-tank guns could be taken across the raging stream to the support of the rifle companies.

As the right forward company was consolidating its objective it was suddenly counter-attacked by a troop of three Mark V Panther tanks supported by two self-propelled guns and about thirty infantry and the situation appeared hopeless.

Under heavy fire from the approaching enemy tanks, Private Smith, showing great initiative and inspiring leadership, led his P.I.A.T. [Projector, Infantry, Anti-Tank gun] Group of two men across an open field to a position from which the P.I.A.T. could best be employed. Leaving one man on the weapon, Private Smith crossed the road with a companion and obtained another P.I.A.T. Almost immediately an enemy tank came down the road firing its machine-guns along the line of the ditches. Private Smith's comrade was wounded. At a range of thirty feet and having to expose himself to the full view of the enemy, Private Smith fired the P.I.A.T. and hit the tank, putting it out of action. Ten German infantry immediately jumped off the back of the tank and charged him with Schmeissers and grenades. Without hesitation Private Smith moved out on the road and with his Tommy gun at point-blank range, killed four Germans and drove the remainder back. Almost immediately another tank opened fire and more enemy infantry closed in on Smith's position. Obtaining some abandoned Tommy gun magazines from a ditch, he steadfastly held his position, protecting his comrade and fighting the enemy with his Tommy gun until they finally gave up and withdrew in disorder.

One tank and both self-propelled guns had been destroyed by this time, but yet another tank swept the area with fire from a longer range. Private Smith,

Mushrooming

The harvesting of edible, wild mushrooms is a popular activity in and around Powell River, and the areas traversed by the Suicide Pass, Smokey's Blue Ridge, and Eagle River trails are all good mushrooming territory. Pine mushrooms and chanterelles are the most popular species in this region, though there are also several other edible species that grow well.

Mushrooms grow in mature forests with mossy forest floors; they do not grow in immature forests or survive in cutblocks. It is important that pickers use the correct techniques to help them to grow back year after year. Here are some mushrooming tips from the BC Forest Service:

- ¤ Pick or cut mushrooms one by one;
- ¤ Do not rake or otherwise disturb the forest floor;
- ¤ Pick only the mushrooms you can use. Broken, over-mature or wormy mushrooms may still be spreading spores;
- ¤ Do not remove or disturb moss layers where more mushrooms are continuously growing;
- ¤ Check the identity of your mushrooms with an experienced harvester, buyer or biologist.

still showing utter contempt for enemy fire, helped his wounded friend to cover and obtained medical aid for him behind a nearby building. He then returned to his position beside the road to await the possibility of a further enemy attack.

No further immediate attack developed, and as a result the battalion was able to consolidate the bridgehead position so vital to the success of the whole operation, which led to the capture of San Giorgio Di Cesena and a further advance to the Ronco River.

Thus, by the dogged determination, outstanding devotion to duty and superb gallantry of this private soldier, his comrades were so inspired that the bridgehead was held firm against all enemy attacks, pending the arrival of tanks and anti-tank guns some hours later.

Later in life Smokey received both the Order of Canada and the Order of British Columbia. In 1995, at the age of 81, Smokey Smith came to Powell River for the grand opening of the trail that leads to the mountain range bearing his name. At the time he was the last living recipient of the Victoria Cross. Before PRPAWS contacted him to ask him to attend the event, he wasn't aware that he had a mountain range, or a trail, named after him.

Cautious Crossing

The Eagle River Trail is the last trail in this section. It is short but picturesque, featuring mossy patches, red huckleberries, plentiful ferns and trees of varying ages. It travels through an area that has already been impacted by harvesting, and logging will likely continue in coming years. Herondell B&B (www.herondell.com) is the official stop for through-hikers needing a break on this part of the SCT, and it's a short hike down a spur off the Eagle River Trail.

Toward the end of the Eagle River Trail you will approach Eagle River (also known as Lois River). This river is dammed, and its flow is normally fairly low, allowing hikers to cross. However, when the gates of the dam are opened, water floods the river and crossing is impossible.

Although sirens are sounded at the dam when gates are opened, hikers may not be able to hear them at the ford of the river, where the trail crosses. For that reason you will be forced to backtrack a few minutes and cross on the Stillwater Main Bridge downstream. See *The Sunshine Coast Trail* guidebook for directions.

(left) The Eagle River Trail is short and sweet; (inset) Pay attention when crossing the river!

Bald Eagle *(Haliaeetus leucocephalus)*

Bald eagles are powerful birds of prey that can live up to 28 years in the wild. They have impressive wingspans of 1.8 to 2.4 metres and weigh between 3 and 6.5 kilograms. Despite the fact that they are the national bird of the United States they were nearly wiped out in that country due to hunting and the use of pesticides like DDT, which accumulate in fish that make up most of the eagle's diet. According to the *National Geographic*'s animals website, "since DDT use was heavily restricted in 1972, eagle numbers have rebounded significantly and have been aided by reintroduction programs. The result is a wildlife success story—the U.S. Fish and Wildlife Service has upgraded the birds from Endangered to Threatened."

Bald eagles are most abundant in Alaska and Canada, and they are commonly seen in and around Powell River. Along the shoreline they can often be observed fishing; if a seal carcass washes up on shore there may be an opportunity to watch dozens of them together at once.

The Last Hurrah
Eagle River to Saltery Bay

¤ Lois Lakeshore Trail
¤ Elephant Lake Trail
¤ West Mount Troubridge Trail
¤ East Mount Troubridge Trail
¤ Rainy Day Lake Trail
¤ Saltery Bay Trail
¤ Fairview Bay Trail

Following the Lakeshore

After climbing down from the Smith Range hikers may be glad to come across the Lois Lakeshore Trail, a picturesque path with minimal elevation gain or loss. As its name suggests this trail follows the shore of Lois Lake.

Near the beginning of the trail you will come across the Lois Lake Dam. Lois River (also known as Eagle River) and Lois Lake were named by Lois Weaver, a former general manager of the Brooks, Scanlon & O'Brien Logging Company at Stillwater. This dam site was first developed in 1929-30 with a temporary log crib dam. The cement dam that still stands there today was built in the 1940s, and took a period of approximately 10 years to complete (in two different stages). It's quite the engineering feat, considering the early equipment that would have been used. The dammed lake that is known as Lois today was formed from two separate lakes, Lois and Gordon Pasha, which became one during the damming process. In the past, people often referred to these two lakes and neighbouring Khartoum Lake as First, Second and Third lakes, or "the Gordon Pashas".

There are several interesting things to notice as you continue along the Lois Lakeshore Trail. Near the dam you will come upon a rusty metal boiler that dates back to early logging days. It was once part of a wood-fired steam donkey that pulled logs out of the lake and loaded them onto trains. Several ravines, which are home to creeks that drain into Lois Lake, are lovely places to stop and do some Forest

(left) Snags left by drowned trees give Lois Lake a dramatic and lonely beauty; (above) An old boiler can be seen along the trail; (right) Several pretty ravines grace Lois Lakeshore.

7 DEC 1940

2358
LOIS CONCRETE DAM
CONCRETE BUCKET
IN G.

Bathing. You will pass two campsites, which are busy in the summer season. The first one is also the start of the Powell Forest Canoe Route. The one further along the trail is known as "Lois Point" and also "Horse Camp," and was constructed by the Back Country Horsemen of BC. If you are lucky, there may be one or two horses in the paddock there.

As you are hiking along, you will have many opportunities to catch glimpses of the lake. You will undoubtedly spot some tree snags sticking out of the water. These are trees that were drowned during the damming process. They remain, ghosts of the past, and make an eerie sight in the early morning mist.

(far left) The Lois Lake Dam as it was being built during the 1940s ~ Powell River Studio photo, courtesy of the Powell River Historical Museum & Archives Society; (left) A view of the dam as it looks today.

Outdoor Recreation User Groups (ORUG)

ORUG is made up of representatives of all the outdoor groups and organizations in the Powell River area. Over the years members of ORUG have worked together to improve trails and their facilities, as well as to deal with political and access issues that affect recreation areas. Although there are sometimes conflicting interests between user groups, it's important that they ultimately cooperate.

Russell Brewer, who is president of the Powell River Cycling Association, and Practices Forester with British Columbia Timber Sales (BCTS), says ORUG denotes credibility to industry stakeholders.

"A group like ORUG that represents all the different user groups is immensely important because industry and BCTS have to listen to them as a stakeholder group. ORUG has got way more clout than each group has individually. They're much more likely to get incorporated into plans officially, and unofficially, at an operational level."

The Powell Forest Canoe Route

The Powell Forest Canoe Route is heaven for outdoor enthusiasts who love to travel by water. Starting at the Branch 41 campsite at Lois Lake, the route crosses eight lakes, including Lois, Horseshoe, Nanton, Ireland, Dodd, Windsor, (Goat and) Powell, and Inland. It has five portages and covers a total distance of 57 kilometres. There are campsites at each stop, with picnic tables, outhouses and fire pits. The Canoe Route was created by BC Forest Service and MacMillan Bloedel (now Western Forest Products), and in 2012 WFP has plans to make the portages, which range in length from 0.7 to 2.4 kilometres, wheelable.

The canoe route is relatively unknown outside of Powell River, and one of its charms is the fact that you can go for days without seeing another soul. Pristine lakes and beautiful scenery will make this a trip to remember. The best time of year to experience the canoe route is June through October. Visit www.canoeingbc.com for more information.

Ascending Again

With the beginning of the Elephant Lake Trail you will once again begin to climb, and this time you are headed to the top of Mount Troubridge and the largest intact stretch of old growth forest along the Sunshine Coast Trail, approximately 11 kilometres. Much of the old growth that starts in the Elephant Lake section and stretches up and over Troubridge is protected within Old Growth Management Areas (OGMAs), and the rest will hopefully be protected into the future as this is an environmentally sensitive area, and home to Marbled Murrelets.

The Elephant Lake Trail is a steady climb through a living tunnel with occasional glimpses of Powell River lowlands, Texada Island and Malaspina Strait in one direction, and Lois Lake in another. You will get a short reprieve from climbing as you reach the picturesque Elephant Lake and follow the trail along the lakeshore for some time.

(left) Sunlight finds its way to the forest floor on the Lois Lakeshore Trail; (right) Canoeing at Nanton Lake.

Everybody needs beauty as well as bread, places to play in and pray in, where nature may heal and give strength to body and soul. ~ *John Muir*

On Top of the World

The West Mount Troubridge Trail continues up and away from Elephant Lake. After an hour and a half you will be delighted to see a cabin that may make you think you are in the Swiss Alps, especially in winter months. This is another delightful area for snowshoeing. The log cabin that sits near the top of Mount Troubridge is truly a work of art. Designed and built by Wiley Hogan in Powell River, individual pieces were flown to the building site by helicopter and reassembled by Wiley, his son, and a PRPAWS crew. The pieces of the cabin went together like a perfect puzzle.

"You couldn't get a cigarette paper in between the logs when it was put together," Jim Stutt says, some wonder still touching his voice.

A Special Place

Troubridge is another section of the SCT that many people name as favourite. It's not as easy to get to as some other parts of the trail, but for that reason it's all the more magical when you get there. Don Krompocker describes it well.

"Troubridge has quickly become another of my favourite spots because of the old growth, and the lack of shrubbery. You walk through that place and it's just like walking on a carpet, surrounded by the biggest trees in the world, but little or no underbrush, only a carpet of moss. Then all of a sudden you pop out and there you are at this beautiful pond and cabin."

Jocelyn and Emily ponds, named after Eagle's daughters, are both located on Mount Troubridge, whose peak is the highest point on the SCT. Once you have enjoyed a rest (or stay) at the cabin, continue through the old growth forest and within half an hour you will come to the summit. The viewpoints from here on in are regular and spectacular.

(left) The gorgeous new cabin near the summit of Mount Troubridge awaits weary hikers; (above) The comments box at Elephant Lake - please leave your name whenever you see one!

PRPAWS Needs Your Voice

All along the Sunshine Coast Trail, as well as at the huts, there are comment boxes with logbooks and pens supplied. This is how PRPAWS tracks the number of people who are using the trail, so be sure to sign in each time you encounter one. Knowing the usage numbers, and how much they are increasing over the years, provides PRPAWS with proof to show that members of the public are out using and enjoying the Sunshine Coast Trail, which helps to raise its profile and value in the eyes of forest stakeholders.

"Live your life each day as you would climb a mountain. An occasional glance toward the summit keeps the goal in mind, but many beautiful scenes are to be observed from each new vantage point." ~ Harold V Melchert

(left) The spectacular view from the summit of Mount Troubridge; (right) Jocelyn Pond is located next to the new cabin on Mount Troubridge.

North American Marbled Muerrelet
(Brachyramphus marmoratus)

Mount Troubridge is important habitat for the Marbled Murrelet, which has been listed as Threatened since 1990 by the Committee on Status of Endangered Wildlife in Canada. These fast-flying seabirds belong to the auk family, but they are unique in the way that, unlike other seabirds in the auk family, they often nest many kilometres from water in trees or on the ground.

Though most of the North American population of Marbled Murrelets is found in Alaska, large numbers breed along the coast of British Columbia, where it appears they are dependent on coastal old-growth type forests, at a range of elevations, for nesting. "Although it is difficult to estimate population sizes or trends, there is concern that populations in BC have declined in areas where extensive logging of coastal forests has taken place. Perhaps their greatest current threat is from the ongoing felling of these forests." (Centre for Wildlife Habitat: Simon Fraser University)

An early Trek de Powell River crew at Sarah Point ~ Margot Glaspey photo

Trek de Powell River

The French may have the Tour de France, but Powell Riverites have the Trek de Powell River. It is not well known yet, but its heyday is coming, Eagle says. The trek is an event that was created to highlight the great distance of the SCT. The idea is to complete the hike from Sarah Point to Saltery Bay on a series of consecutive days with a designated starting date. When the annual trek started in the mid-'90s, hikers did as much of the trail as they could each year, given the circumstances and trail conditions at the time. Lita Biron is a long-time member of the PRPAWS executive. She was part of the first Trek de Powell River.

"Eagle and Scott tried to dissuade me from going because I was small and didn't look so tough," she laughs fondly. "Eagle would work on me, then Scott would phone me and work on me, but there was no way I was going to renege! I did the trek about three times I guess. The first time we had really heavy packs because we carried everything we needed for the full nine days. The second time it was seven days. We didn't have to carry as much then because people came in and brought our stuff every day to our camp.

"I had a lot of dreams while I was out there – about things I didn't do, like falling off mountains. It really impacted me. I remember being at Granite Lake, and I was changing into my bathing suit to go swimming. I thought one of the dogs was up there with me; I heard a noise in the bush across the road. I called the dogs but they weren't there, and I realized it was a bear! I took off down that road so fast – but that bear was as scared as I was!"

After five or six years the event petered out as it was difficult to find people willing to commit a number of days to being on the trail in one stretch. However, with growing interest in the trail and the new huts in place, PRPAWS hopes to revive the trek in the future.

American black bear

(Ursus americanus)

American black bears are North America's smallest and most common bear. They can be found in all Canadian provinces except Prince Edward Island. They are approximately 1.2 to 2 metres from nose to tail and 0.5 to 1 metre at shoulder height. They have small eyes, rounded ears, a long snout, a short tail, and light gray skin. Their fur is shaggy or sleek, depending upon the season. On the west coast they may be brown, cinnamon, black, and occasionally white in colour.

The majority of a black bear's diet consists of plant matter – berries, fruit, grasses, nuts and buds are favourites. They also eat insects such as bees, yellow-jackets, ants and their larvae. Black bears will fish for salmon at night, as their black fur is easily spotted by salmon in the daytime. Occasionally they eat small or young deer or elk.

Black bears along the Fairview Bay Trail ~ Eagle Walz photo

Attacks on humans by black bears are uncommon. If you do encounter one, it will likely be as frightened as you are, and most often it will run away. Bear sightings along the Sunshine Coast Trail are rare, but as hikers are passing through their home territory, sometimes they do happen.

According to the North American Bear Center, if you see a black bear the best thing to do is speak calmly and back away slowly. Doing this "identifies you as a person, shows that you are non-threatening, and gives the bear space...Those are polite actions that respect a black bear's comfort zone and help ease its anxiety. It is the gentle way to separate. More aggressive action would be more likely to increase a black bear's anxiety and send it running." (North American Bear Center)

The Final Descent

The East Mount Troubridge Trail heads down steadily, and steeply in sections. You are on the home stretch now, on the long descent to Saltery Bay and the end of the SCT. Be sure to watch your footing, but don't forget to take a break and look up every once in a while; there are several scenic vistas to enjoy, and glimpses of Rainy Day Lake below. You will pass through quite a few old growth sections. Appreciate the buffer that was left for the trail when this area was logged in recent years. It protected some giants, so keep your eyes open for them, and especially a yellow cedar more than 1.5 metres in diameter, which is likely among the oldest trees growing on Canada's west coast.

Near the end of the trail you will also have the opportunity to see a cutblock growing back into a young forest. Enjoy the panoramic views; Jervis Inlet, Nelson Island, Hotham Sound and the Sechelt Peninsula are all laid out before you.

Hailstones and Rainy Days

The name of the next trail section may not inspire warmth, but keep in mind that rainy days make things grow green! Another impressive stand of old growth and more views are highlights of the Rainy Day Trail section, but the icing on the cake is Rainy Day Lake itself, and another hut that is located right at the lake. The lowland area the lake sits in is known for unpredictable weather conditions.

"You often get funny weather there, like hailstones and snow," Eagle says, hence the name of the lake, and that of Hailstone Bluffs, along this trail. Nevertheless, if you are caught by inclement weather, there is now a place to take shelter. The Rainy Day Lake hut was built by PRPAWS with the help of the Powell River Rotary Club. If it's a hot day, walk around the lake on the old logging road to enjoy the swimming dock there. There is also a campsite below the hut at Rainy Day Lake.

(left) Eagle makes his way down East Mount Troubridge Trail, with a view of Jervis Inlet ahead; (right) The ferry leaving Saltery Bay; (insets) The hut at Rainy Day Lake.

The human spirit needs places where nature has not been rearranged by the hand of man.
~ Author Unknown

Jervis Inlet

Jervis Inlet, located about 95 kilometres northwest of Vancouver, is a main inlet along the BC Coast. It was named Jervis by George Vancouver during his 1791-95 expedition in honour of Rear Admiral Sir John Jervis. One of four subgroups of the Sechelt First Nation, xénichen, once lived at the head of the inlet, near the mouth of the Skwawka River. From there it stretches 77 kilometres to its opening in the Strait of Georgia near Texada Island. It is the deepest fjord on the BC coast, with a maximum depth of 732 metres (*Encyclopedia of BC*).

Logging and commercial fishing developed in this area around the early 1900s, and a fish-processing plant was located in Saltery Bay, which was named for the fish saltery there. Now Saltery Bay is best known as the home of the BC Ferries Saltery Bay terminal and the start/finish of the Sunshine Coast Trail!

A Feast for the Eyes

The last section of the SCT is a Choose Your Own Adventure: Saltery Bay Trail, or Fairview Bay Trail?

The Saltery Bay Trail takes a more direct route down to Saltery Bay and the end of the SCT; much of it was built on top of an old logging road, called Marquis' Road after the local logger who built it. It descends relatively quickly down to Saltery Bay. Before you head down, however, there is a loop at the top of the trail that you will take you out to Blue Grouse Ridge, and a dazzling viewpoint from which you can see Freil Falls.

(left and right) Spectacular views from the Saltery Bay Trail; (above, inset) Salal is commonly found on this trail section.

(above) The hut at Fairview Bay; (right, inset) The Fairview Bay Hut was the first to be constructed, and was used as a prototype for all the others; (far right) The Fairview Bay trail follows the shoreline in part, and is consequently a special part of the Sunshine Coast Trail.

Beautiful Bay

Overall the Fairview Bay section is much more scenic, and the better choice for your final hike down to Saltery Bay. This final section of the SCT is lovely because it takes you back down to the water's edge and allows you to follow the coastline, enjoying attractive views of the water a lot of the way. For the most part the Fairview Bay Trail runs through an Old Growth Management Area (OGMA) that stretches from Saltery Bay to Fairview Bay, with the exception of a couple of interruptions.

The development of this OGMA has been recently negotiated between PRPAWS and British Columbia Timber Sales (BCTS).

"Years ago we promoted the idea of having an OGMA all the way from Saltery Bay to Fairview Bay along the shore and up from the shore," Eagle says. "A small part of the trail apparently was just outside of it, and so they suggested that we relocate that part of the trail into the OGMA, which is lower down. They actually did the work themselves, we didn't have to do it." Many of the relocations that have been necessary or desirable along various sections of the SCT, however, have been done by PRPAWS. "We are actually building the SCT a second time in many sections," Eagle continues. "It's probably not just 180 kilometres – it's probably more like 230 by now. BCTS has been really good in maintaining the parameters that were agreed to under the Stillwater Timberlands Pilot Project, and in the other areas that they're responsible for, they appear to be willing to provide the same considerations."

The hut at Fairview Bay was the very first one to be built; all the other huts and cabins are based on this prototype. It is visible from the water and will certainly attract visitors from the water in its own right. The bay is sheltered and suitable for swimming or anchoring a boat. At the northern end a creek runs down into the sea, and you can find a supply of potable fresh water there year-round. A grant from the Powell River Community Foundation allowed for the building of several benches along this gorgeous stretch of trail, so take the time to sit and enjoy the views.

The Dream Continues

And in the End...

Most people who visit or live in Powell River appreciate the area's beauty. This land of plenty is rich with dazzling ocean views, easy access to freshwater lakes, stunning mountain backdrops, and a backyard of green forests. There has long been a struggle here between tourism and resource-extraction industries, a tug-of-war between keeping this place pristine, and supporting parts of the economy that have traditionally allowed people to work and live here. A 180-kilometre trail that runs through land controlled by a number of stakeholders, including British Columbia Timber Sales (BCTS), Tla'Amin First Nation, Powell River Community Forest, Western Forest Products (WFP), Island Timberlands Limited Partnership (ITLP) and other private landowners, then, is ambitious, to say the least.

Managing Many Interests

Russell Brewer, Practices Forester with BCTS in Powell River, says he thinks most people at BCTS are supportive of the Sunshine Coast Trail and its initiatives, but some concern lies in the fact that it spans such a large area. PRPAWS' stated goal is to have the whole 180-kilometre trail buffered, so that it will eventually become a ribbon of old growth. "Industry views that as a relatively large impact," Russell says. "I think for the most part the way we'll manage the sections that are on Crown land, which we are responsible for, is to try to locate the trail in wildlife tree patches or retention areas, or Old Growth Management Areas. We'll try and buffer the trail where we can, and minimize road crossings, so it is managed."

Stuart Glen, Operations Planner with WFP says the two interests of timber harvesting and tourism don't have to be at odds, and that recreation is one of many values considered when timber harvesting is being planned.

"We've been entrusted to manage the land in our Tree Farm Licence, and there are a whole lot of values associated with it – from the wildlife, the biodiversity, the economic values, et cetera. A big part of managing the forest is incorporating all of those together. We're fortunate to have the recreation opportunities that we have in this area – it's part of the area. Managing for it fits in with everything else that we do."

A Growing Industry

Today tourism is a growing industry on the Upper Sunshine Coast. Though its development has been hindered due to relative isolation and the expense it takes to get here, what Powell River has to offer is special, and it has enormous potential. In terms of outdoor recreation – especially when it comes to the Sunshine Coast Trail, which runs through property controlled by so many stakeholders – that potential is best realized when all parties work together.

"If we hadn't worked together, and showed some success in doing so," Eagle says, "we would have long ago stopped what we were doing. In a small community such as this, you have to live with each other. I'm an optimist and I like to get along with other people, because to me much more is achieved by cooperating. We struggle – we do struggle in trying to protect the trail and its surroundings, but there are good working relationships between PRPAWS and the other parties that may have competing interests."

Those good working relationships are a result of the direction, guidance and diplomacy of the man who has played such an instrumental role in the creation of the Sunshine Coast Trail. Eagle is respected and admired by all who have worked with him – whether they are friends, fellow PRPAWS members, or members of the forestry industry.

"I really like Eagle's approach," Russell says. "He is very diplomatic and moderate, and that gets you much further than screaming and stomping on the table. I think Eagle is respected by everybody because he's reasonable in his demands."

The way Eagle inspires others is expressed well by Bob Davey, one of the newest members of the PRPAWS board.

(left) Ron Diprose, better known as "Dipper," does some trail maintenance on the West Tin Hat Trail; (right) Blue skies and gnarly trees along the Scout Mountain Trail.

"Listening to the way that Eagle deals with people – the loggers, for instance – he's so gentle, and not confrontational. He's a gentleman in the true sense of the word. I find that an amazing trait that I'd love to develop more for myself."

Eagle's wife, Laura, who knows best how dedicated he has been to the development and promotion of the trail over the years, says that Eagle has gained a lot from the experiences he has had.

"Eagle is a people person and people really like him. He draws people to him, but I think he's become more of a negotiator and more of a leader over the years. People look to him and listen to what he has to say. He has had to become a skilled negotiator, and that's very tricky because you want to maintain relationships with people who may not be on your side, and he's very good at doing that."

Though he never let the trail come between him and his family, or his work as a schoolteacher, Eagle has been completely dedicated to it all these years, Laura continues. "He's totally passionate about it, and you can see that it feeds him. It makes him the really wonderful person that he is, the love he has for it."

A PRPAWS Community

Over the years, more than 500 people have been involved in PRPAWS, some in a very hands-on way, others in more supportive roles. The Sunshine Coast Trail project resonates with people and makes them want to get involved. From buying a membership to trail clearing and hut building, every single donation of time and resources is appreciated.

"It's critically important to involve people over time," Eagle says. "Whoever wants to join in is welcome to because every contribution helps to move the project closer to the standard that we aspire to, and that is world-class. We will only get there with the participation of a large pool of people to draw on – some repeatedly, others just once or twice. It is a monumental task and it requires a community to do this. Without that community the trail would have long ago reverted to wilderness, and gone back to being logged merrily with no one the wiser, or caring about it. When you have a trail people are able to see the beauty of the backcountry. Then they can say, 'Hey, maybe one per cent of this ought to be for us; even half a per cent would be nice.' So that's why it's so important to make everyone feel welcome, and whatever level of participation they contribute is valued."

And besides, it's fun!

"We have such a good time going out together – it's just fun," Scott says. "You are out with your buddies; there are no bosses. There's no one telling you that you have to do things a certain way, unless it's the carpenter and it really does have to be done that way. For the most part if you don't like a job, you just go away and find another job."

Bob moved to Powell River recently and has been involved with the group for the past couple of years. He got invited out to a work party, and has never looked back.

"People have to get out there to understand it," he says. "You can't explain it to someone. Eagle will tell you the first time you come out on a work party, there are no rules. You break when you want to break, you relax when you want to relax, and you work when you want to work. No one looks at you sideways if you decide you want to go and sit down for however long. Or if you see something off in the distance and you want to go explore it, you go ahead. We're not in a work camp, we're here to enjoy the outdoors and enjoy our surroundings. There's always something for every level of ability. You can grab a pair of clippers and walk along the trail and clip some salal, or if you feel up to it you can grab a sledgehammer and beat on a rock for a while." He laughs. "Although it's hard to get hold of the sledgehammer because there are a couple of guys who are sledgehammer hogs and like to break rocks. Everyone works at their own pace and their own comfort level and things just get done. By the end of the day it doesn't feel like you've been working.

(left) Eagle at the top of East Mount Troubridge Trail; (right) Terry Roberts works on some new stairs on the Fairview Bay trail section.

I believe that there is a subtle magnetism in Nature, which, if we unconsciously yield to it, will direct us aright. ~ Henry David Thoreau

"There is a secret there and it's all wrapped up in Krompocker singing and Eagle joking around, and everyone having fun. When you get home you might be physically tired but you don't feel like it was work. You were just out playing in the woods; it's a big huge sandbox and you were out there playing."

Looking to the Future

The building of the huts and the addition of consistent and noticeable trail markers in both directions that are being put in place on the Sunshine Coast Trail are lifting it to a new level, ever closer to that world-class mark. The possibilities for the value the trail could provide to the community of Powell River are just beginning to reveal themselves.

In 2011 the Sunshine Coast Trail was featured in more than 20 national magazines, newspapers and other media. As well, it is seeing a definite increase in traffic from locals and visitors, Don says. "There are more and more families, and more and more young people out there hiking that trail, and people who are maybe not so young. People are out there doing just the portion that they want to do, or the piece that they love. They go out there and sit at the shelter, or on a bench, and they enjoy it. That's the satisfaction we get out of it."

The trail is going to be a huge economic driver for this community, he continues. "Despite what the politicians say, new mills and industry may be a great thing, but that hasn't happened yet. The economic drivers that we have in Powell River are going to be in tourism."

Scott seconds that. "If you think about why people live here, it's not because of the mill, it's because it's a neat place to live, and a lot of the reason for that is the lifestyle that you live, especially if you are an outdoor person. If you like the outdoors, this is the best place in the world to come."

(left) A peek at Lois Lake from the Lois Lakeshore Trail; (right) Strolling along the Mowat Bay Trail.

As newcomers to the community Bob and his wife Angie see it through fresh eyes.

"I think we've got something extremely special in this trail," Bob says. "Just being out there and discovering the different types of forest and terrain blows me away. One thing Angie and I always say is, 'We get to live here', and I get those moments on the trail constantly where you turn a corner and it's like, 'Oh my God, this is fantastic!'"

The use of the trail by visitors is important to its success, Eagle says. "It's a huge benefit to have people from elsewhere come and show their level of appreciation for what there is here. That helps local people to see what they have."

When Scott thinks about the vision for the trail, he compares it to some of the great walks he and Margot went on in New Zealand.

"It would be really nice to have this trail well known. I look at the West Coast Trail, which has been called world-class. The Sunshine Coast Trail is two-and-a-half times as long and it's going to have way more amenities, and if the community buys into this, that's only going to increase. What happened in New Zealand was that the people who ran every facility were all cooperating and communicating. They were hooked into this web, so they were helping each other tremendously. You think of all the B&Bs and all the hotels, and all the eating establishments, and the people who are going to make money moving people's cars around, delivering food and supplies – this could be quite an amazing thing. People were quite willing to pay $30 per night just to have a warm, dry place to sleep. Those huts were more than paying for themselves. Powell River could see the same benefits from our trail and the facilities on it."

(left) Shufflers along the Marathon Trail; (right) A secluded spot on Fairview Bay Trail.

"If you like the outdoors, this is the best place in the world to come."

The Dream Continues

Shortly after they started work on the Sunshine Coast Trail Eagle and Scott realized that it would eventually have to evolve into something that would be passed on to the community. It needs to be the right time, however, and that time hasn't come yet.

"We've tried it a couple of times, but the community hasn't been ready," Eagle says. "We think that sooner or later it will be. People are starting to see that this recreation and tourism business is bringing people to Powell River."

When the time does come it will be like seeing a child spreading her wings, he continues.

"I compare it to raising children. You do the best you can and then one day they leave home. They have to, and you just have to let them go. They will develop into whatever they will develop into. We have had a 20-year plan for the trail that is drawing near fruition and that vision is to save old growth and to have areas of biodiversity in the region, to help animals and nature survive in conditions that you might have found 100-150 years ago or longer, and to provide opportunities for people to work and play here."

The Sunshine Coast Trail is more than a trail, more than a beautiful place to walk. It's the representation of a dream and the spirit of a group of people who believe it's worthwhile to protect the forests of this area and the animals that live within their boundaries. This story is far from over; it's one that will be remembered when the Sunshine Coast Trail has achieved world-class status and people are coming from around the globe to discover the delights it has to offer. This is a vision for the future that is happening now. So lace up your hiking boots, and grab your hiking stick (or a pair of work gloves) and become part of the story.

(left) A massive tree on the Lost Lake Trail; (right) Scott and Eagle enjoy fall colours along the Fairview Bay Trail.

Acknowledgements

There are many people who helped in the production of this book, but a few whose important contributions made it possible.

My husband, Matt Larocque. Always in the background, Matt has been constantly supportive, as always providing me with whatever I need. Whether that was a hiking buddy, a navigator, a cook while I was too busy to think about eating, or a hug. I am full of gratitude for him every day.

My talented friend and the map artist for this book, Melany Hallam. A self-taught illustrator, graphic designer and writer, Melany has been involved in art and writing from an early age, but has only become focussed on illustration in the past few years—and is now wondering what took her so long to get there. Her work can be seen on her company website at www.maywooddesign.com.

My parents, David and Mandy Levez. The constant support, help and encouragement they offered throughout this project, is one in a long list of examples of the ways they have shown that they believe in me throughout my life. Thanks guys!

My friends, Kate and Doug Cooper, who spent many a day hiking with me, and provided invaluable moral support throughout the writing of this book.

My friend, Eagle Walz. Ever generous with his time, Eagle spent countless hours explaining the details of the past 20 years, hooking me up with the people I needed to talk to, and reading - and rereading - the drafts of this book. As anyone who has met him knows, he is a gentle, inspiring man - one I feel lucky to call my friend.

My friend, Kuxy Doell, who was always ready and willing to go for a hike (no matter how hard the hike was, or how much it was raining!) And of course Zulu and Alley who kept us on the right track and made sure we didn't spot any wildlife.

Published by Lens & Quill Designs
8581 Myrtle Point Drive, Powell River, BC, Canada V8A OH1
Tel: 604-487-1945

Editing by Eagle Walz, Laura Walz and Matt Larocque
Layout and Design by Emma Levez Larocque
Map artwork by Melany Hallam of Maywood Design (www.maywooddesign.com)
Photographs by Emma Levez Larocque, except where noted otherwise
Writing by Emma Levez Larocque
Proofreading (all) by Eagle Walz, Laura Walz, Matt Larocque
Proofreading (selected pieces) by Teedie Kagume, Linda Scheiber, Stuart Glen, Scott Glaspey, Russell Brewer, Rudi Van Zwaaij, and John Louie.
Transcribing by Mandy Levez
Research Assistance: Eagle Walz; Scott and Margot Glaspey; Laura Walz; Don Krompocker; Teedie Kagume and Fran Cudworth (Powell River Historical Museum & Archives); Rudi Van Zwaaij and Dave Florence (Powell River Forestry Museum), Blake Fougere and Russell Brewer (BC Timber Sales), Stuart Glen (Western Forest Products); Linda Scheiber; John Louie; Clint Williams; Roy Hewitt; Roger Taylor; Jim Stutt; Bob Davey; Lita Biron; Monty Tyrwhitt-Drake; Al Baronas (ICET); and Ean Jackson.

Resources: *The Sunshine Coast Trail* by Eagle Walz,; *Plants of the Pacific Northwest Coast: Washington, Oregon, British Columbia & Alaska* by Jim Pojar and Andy MacKinnon; *Boats, Bucksaws and Blisters* by Bill Thompson; *Once Upon a Stump* by Bill Thompson; *Powell River's First 50 Years* edited by Al Alsgard; *Pulp, Paper and People* by Karen Southern and Peggy Bird; *The Eden Express* by Mark Vonnegut; and a variety of newspaper articles and websites (as noted in the text).

Copyright © Lens & Quill Designs 2011

Thanks to my hiking buddies: Matt Larocque; Kate Saunders Cooper; Kuxy Doell (with Alley and Zulu); Doug Cooper; Tara Chernoff; Christopher Chernoff; Jeffrey Chernoff; Melany Hallam; and Kate Spanks. And to Oceanview Helicopters, James Mode, Derek Johnson and Melany Hallam, and Malcolm Prentice for their roadside (and mountainside) assistance. Special thanks to Mandy and David Levez whose support helped to make this book possible.

Cover photo: Eagle Walz and Scott Glaspey on Fairview Bay Trail.
Dedication page photo: Eagle Walz and Scott Glaspey at the top of Tin Hat Mountain ~ Margot Glaspey photo.
Section title page photos: pp.15 This way to the Sunshine Coast Trail!; pp. 27 Winter freezes one of the small falls on Appleton Creek Trail; pp. 51 Lost Lake; pp. 70 On the way into the March Lake Trail; pp. 97 A beautiful day for sailing near Fairview Bay; pp. 115 Ambling along the Appleton Canyon Trail.

ISBN 978-0-9780654-4-7
Printed in Canada by Friesens Corporation.